Paris
by Boat

A Boatowners' Guide to
the Seine and Paris Canals

David Jefferson

ADLARD COLES NAUTICAL

London

For my brother, Richard
1946–1997

Published 1997 by Adlard Coles Nautical
an imprint of A & C Black (Publishers) Ltd
35 Bedford Row, London WC1R 4JH

Copyright © David Jefferson 1997

ISBN 0-7136-4629-2

A CIP catalogue record for this book is available from
the British Library.

Typeset in 11 on 12pt Goudy
Printed and bound in Great Britain by
Cromwell Press, Melksham, Wiltshire

Acknowledgements

The author wishes to thank Ian Macfarlane and Julie Draper for the
river plans; Gérard Vionnet of the Port Autonome de Rouen for
permission to reproduce the tidal graphs of the Lower Seine; APEX
Cartographie for permission to reproduce the Paris plan on page 61; the
Chambre de Commerce et d'Industrie du Havre for permission to use
the photograph of the Pont de Normandie; the Comité Départemental
de Tourisme de Seine-Maritime for permission to use the photographs
on page 27.

Unless otherwise indicated, all photographs are by the author.

Contents

Part III *The Canals of Paris*

Part IV *Sectional maps of the Seine*
from the estuary to Paris

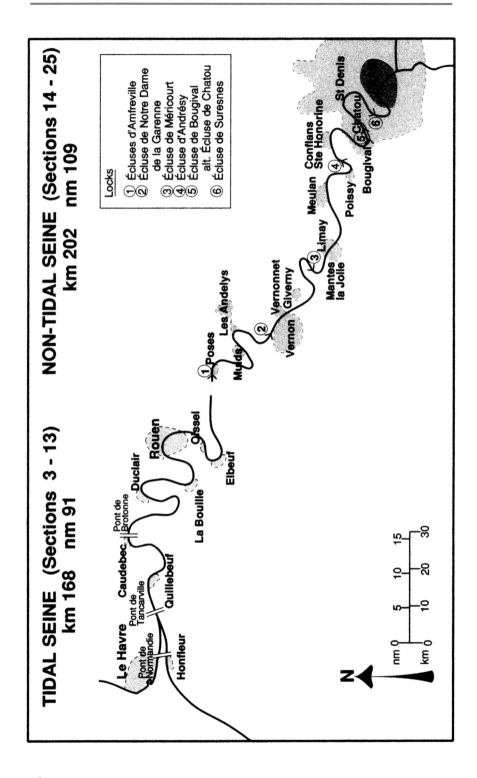

TIDAL SEINE (Sections 3 - 13) km 168 nm 91

NON-TIDAL SEINE (Sections 14 - 25) km 202 nm 109

Locks
① Écluses d'Amfreville
② Écluse de Notre Dame de la Garenne
③ Écluse de Méricourt
④ Écluse d'Andrésy
⑤ Écluse de Bougival alt. Écluse de Chatou
⑥ Écluse de Suresnes

Le Havre
Pont de Normandie
Honfleur
Pont de Tancarville
Quillebeuf
Caudebec
Pont de Brotonne
Duclair
Rouen
La Bouille
Ossel
Elbeuf

Poses ①
Muids
Les Andelys
Vernonnet
Giverny
Vernon ②
Mantes la Jolie
Limay ③
Meulan
Conflans Ste Honorine
Poissy ④
Bougival ⑤ Chatou
St Denis
⑥

N

nm 0   5   10   15
km 0   10   20   30

·····················◆·····················

Introduction

There is something special about entering Paris, and viewing the sights from your own boat. Motoring under the famous bridges, some of which have spanned the Seine since the 14th century, is an unforgettable experience. Prominent amongst the many famous landmarks is the vast building housing the Louvre Museum, with the Eiffel Tower on the left bank. The boat glides beneath the Pont Neuf, in the shadows of Notre Dame Cathedral on the Île de la Cité. A mere 3 km upriver of Notre Dame is the capital's attractive yacht harbour – the Port de Plaisance de Paris-Arsenal, just off the Place de la Bastille.

It would be wrong to give the impression that the only highlight of a cruise up the Seine is the arrival in Paris. The 365 km (197 nm) of waterways include seven locks; upriver of the first of these are miles of backwaters to explore, behind the Seine's numerous islands. There are delightful well-established stopping-off places, or the boatowner can simply drop anchor in some secluded spot for the night, or for a couple of hours around lunchtime.

For those making their first cruise to Paris, the spectacular scenery comes as something of a surprise. Once beyond the Seine estuary, the

The curiously named Pont Neuf is the oldest bridge in Paris.

1

river winds through valleys below forests and chalk cliffs. In other sections, often lined with poplars, the fields stretch into the distance. There are many of the distinctive Normandy farmhouses, and the occasional magnificent château. Parts of the river resemble the more fashionable frontages of the upper Thames, with weeping willows, boat-houses and water-skiing. For mile after mile, the crew will have these delightful surroundings virtually to themselves, apart from a passing barge or, below Rouen, the occasional merchant ship.

A cruise to and from Paris is possible in most pleasure craft capable of crossing the Channel (see sections 3 and 14 for maximum dimensions). Masts of sailing yachts have to be removed before entering Rouen, but this presents no problem (see section 4). Boats with modest engine power (10 bhp/5 kn) are not precluded from a cruise between Le Havre and Paris. They can still complete the 365 km from the sea to the capital in five to six days, without the passage becoming something of an endurance test.

The Paris cruise is certainly not restricted to those fortunate enough to have many weeks available for cruising during the summer. With careful planning, boatowner and crew can cruise the Seine over a three-week period, and still have plenty of time for sightseeing in Paris, perhaps venturing along more waterways, including sections of the canals of Paris which are covered in Part III.

The best-laid plans can always be frustrated by the weather, delaying the Channel crossing. For small craft, there is much to be said for getting the boat over to the other side, perhaps the weekend before the start of the cruise proper. Crossing over from the south coast of England, there are many excellent yacht harbours either side of the Seine estuary, some of which are conveniently situated at passenger ferry ports. These harbours are described briefly in sections 1 and 2.

PART I
Tidal Seine

between the Seine approaches and the first lock at Bas-de-Poses

1 Seine approaches (harbours to the east):
Le Tréport • Dieppe • St Valery-en-Caux
• Fécamp • Le Havre

To the east of Le Havre, steep chalk cliffs dominate the 70 miles of coast-line, almost reaching the Somme. In the gaps in the cliffs are four yacht harbours. They are, with distances from Le Havre in nautical miles, Le Tréport (68), Dieppe (56), St Valery-en-Caux (39) and Fécamp (25). These ports are described below, along with basic navigation details; readers should refer to pilot books of the area to obtain more detailed information.

Le Tréport

Sixty miles across the Channel from Eastbourne, Le Tréport is a lively, long-established holiday resort, attracting many visitors from Paris. There is a popular bathing beach, a casino, and many restaurants lining the quay-side. The port has undergone considerable change due to a £25 million development programme. A new lock has been built, giving the fishing boats and pleasure craft access to basins originally used as water-pounds.

A century ago, Le Tréport was linked by canal to Eu – then an impor-tant commercial port, used by large sailing ships. Part of the development plan provides for the opening up of this canal, and craft with a height above the waterline of less than 6 m will be able to travel the 2.6 km to the ancient town, where there is still a *quai maritime*, and the Café de la Marine sign, around the pool where the sailing ships turned. Boats with fixed masts can cover about two-thirds of the distance, whence it is a 10–15 minute walk into town. Yachts have to stand off the drying entrance to Le Tréport until there is sufficient water to enter the lock which is worked four hours either side of HW.

Dieppe

Anyone who has merely disembarked at Dieppe's car ferry terminal, and driven on to distant holiday resorts, will be pleasantly surprised with what this town has to offer. Visiting craft now have their own harbour off the quay previously used by the Newhaven–Dieppe ferry. The resort has a long beach, flanked by a wide promenade overlooked by large hotels, a casino and an imposing castle. The *vieux quartier*, most of which survived World War Two, consists of narrow, cobbled streets packed with excellent restaurants, bars and interesting shops. The small craft harbour is accessible at all states of tide, and barriers around the pontoons protect boats from the swell that enters the harbour in strong onshore winds.

St-Valery-en-Caux

The approach to St-Valery-en-Caux involves making for the only gap in the cliffs hereabouts, with the town situated at the head of a long ravine. Access to the yacht basin, which has berths for nearly 600 craft, is through a lock, which operates HW ± 2¼ (day) and HW ± ½ (night), and a lifting bridge which is raised on the hour and half-hour over these periods. The *Avant Port* dries and, particularly in onshore winds (W–NE), care should be taken approaching the port (no earlier than HW –3). The yacht basin is right in the centre of this attractive holiday resort.

Fécamp

The holiday resort of Fécamp has long been popular with visiting British boats. From the Nab Tower, off the eastern approaches to the Solent, Fécamp is a passage of 76 nm, and nearer than Le Havre (84 nm). Brighton to Fécamp is only 68 nm. Viewed from the top of the cliffs the way in to Fécamp, between the breakwaters, can look intimidating, with an unbroken sand bar across the entrance. At low water springs there is only 1.5 m here. Boats should approach from the south, as there is a particularly shallow patch just north of the northern breakwater. The entrance presents no problems, except in strong winds (force 7 or above) between W and NW.

The marina, where 30 of the 530 places are for visitors, is to starboard on entering. The pontoons, connected to the Quai Vauban, are overlooked by a star-shaped building that houses the Capitainerie, showers and the hospitable yacht club (Société des Regates de Fécamp). On the other side of the Quai Vauban is the promenade and bathing beach, packed with holidaymakers during the season. Fécamp's main tourist attraction is the Palais Bénédictine, where the famous liqueur is blended. Open daily to the public, several of the palace's halls, which house the distillery, can be viewed. There is also an art museum and modern art gallery on the premises. On completion of a tour of the Palais, visitors are invited to sample the product, which is made up of a blend using 27 plants and herbs, dating back to a 16th century recipe used by the local monks.

The outer pontoon berths for small craft visiting Fécamp can sometimes be uncomfortable in strong onshore winds; the inner Bassin Berigny may prove a more attractive alternative (opens between HW –2 and HW). There are several restaurants overlooking the Avant Port.

Le Havre

For many boatowners, Le Havre will be the starting place for a Seine cruise. The ferry terminal is about 15 minutes' walk from the yacht harbour. With regular sailings to and from Portsmouth, Le Havre is a particularly convenient place for changing crews. Owners of small boats, planning to cross the Channel before the cruise proper, to avoid the frustrations of a departure delayed by bad weather, will find Le Havre an excellent place to leave the boat for a few days.

The 1200 berth marina at Le Havre is a sharp turn to port, having passed through the main entrance to the Avant Port. Visiting boats lie both sides of the outer pontoon. Anyone unfamiliar with the town, and setting out from the marina without a map or guide, might well walk for 20 minutes and fail to find a single shop, as there is no immediately apparent centre to Le Havre.

As France's second port, founded early in the 16th century by King François I as an alternative to silted-up Harfleur and Honfleur, Le Havre was flattened by allied bombing in World War Two. The French, giving priority to rebuilding the town after the war in the shortest time possible, turned to Auguste Perret, an architect who was pioneering the use of reinforced concrete. The result is unlike anything else seen in France, with great blocks of flats, wide straight roads and one of the largest city squares in Europe – the Place de l'Hôtel-de-Ville. There are many examples of modern architecture, like St Joseph's Church, just behind the marina, which is glass with a great tower block for a spire. The Oscar Niemeyer House of Culture, with galleries and a theatre, is contained within a concrete dome-shaped building, with a baby one alongside.

There are many shops, restaurants, bars and banks around the Hôtel-de-Ville, about 20 minutes' walk from the marina. There is a supermarket closer to the boats (from the Capitainerie, cross the Boulevard Clemenceau, making for St Joseph's Church, turn left down the Rue Augustin Normand, and the supermarket is on the right). To the left, in Rue Augustin Normand is ADMT, the nearest marine engineer. Beyond the church and the hospital, in the Place des Halles, are the Halles Centrales – an excellent, covered market, predominantly selling food and drink.

···················◆·····················

2 Seine approaches (harbours to the west): Ouistreham • Caen • Port Guillaume • Deauville• Honfleur

In total contrast to the high cliffs to the east of Le Havre, the coastline to the west is flat and almost featureless, with sandbanks extending several miles out to sea. This coastline includes several yacht harbours conveniently close to the entrance to the Chenal de Rouen, in the Seine estuary. They are, with distances in nautical miles from the outer mark (Ratier NW channel buoy), the ferry terminal and yacht harbour at Ouistreham (15), Dives-sur-Mer (11), Deauville (5) and, on the west side of the Seine estuary, Honfleur (6.5 upstream).

Ouistreham

If Le Havre cannot be reached on passage from the west, preparatory to a Seine cruise, a convenient alternative might be Ouistreham, with a regular ferry service to and from Portsmouth. The deepwater approach channel, dredged across the sandbanks for the ferry, is well-marked with buoys and beacon towers; the lighthouse and illuminated leading lights are often clearly visible by day. The lock, giving access to the Ouistreham–Caen canal and the yacht harbour, is worked HW ± 3, between 0600 and 2200. For pleasure craft, there is a waiting pontoon to port, past the ferry terminal, but be warned that, if used for any other purpose apart from waiting for the lock to open, the fines can be enormous.

The yacht harbour here is excellent. Chandlery and fuel are conveniently close to the marina, and there is a grocer, butcher and restaurant around the square on the other side of the lock. There are also stalls selling fresh fish. It is 3 km, again across the lock, in the direction of the ferry terminal, to Ouistreham's holiday resort at Riva-Bella, where there is a long sandy beach lined with bathing huts.

Caen

Anyone with a day or two to spare might consider continuing up the canal for another 16 km to the fine city of Caen. The notice-board outside the yacht club should be consulted for bridge-opening times. There are two openings daily (with an additional opening on Friday and Sunday evenings). One of the two daily openings, usually around 9 am, has to be paid for, and is primarily for commercial traffic. The other

Caen's yacht harbour is right in the centre of the city.

opening, free of charge, is linked with high water, so that craft descending from Caen can arrive with only a short wait for the lock opening. The notice displayed outside the yacht club (or VHF Ch 9 during office hours) indicates when craft, making the passage to Caen, should be at the first of the lifting bridges (5 km from the yacht harbour). It is recommended that boats leave the marina in good time, arriving at the bridge at least ten minutes before the scheduled opening.

This was the site of intense fighting in World War Two, when glider-borne commandos were landed behind enemy lines before the D-Day offensive. They successfully captured and held the bridge, which was subsequently renamed Pegasus, after the insignia of the Airborne Regiment. A museum devoted to the raid, along with the original bridge and the faithfully preserved Café Gondrée, attracted many visitors. In 1994 the bridge was replaced by a replica of greater dimensions, to enable larger cruise ships to reach Caen (including the Royal Yacht *Britannia*, which visited Caen as part of the 50th Anniversary D-Day celebrations). Several yachts will usually assemble near the bridge, and then race through at the first opportunity. This achieves very little, because progress through the subsequent three opening bridges is dictated by the progress of the slowest boat in the convoy.

It takes about 1¼ hours to reach Caen, and the pontoons in the Bassin St-Pierre, in the centre of the town. Established in the 12th century by William the Conqueror and his wife Mathilde, Princess of Flanders,

9

Belgium and Normandy, much of Caen was bombed in World War Two, but the two 11th-century abbeys remain. The Abbaye des Hommes was built by William the Conqueror, and the Abbaye aux Dames was built by Mathilde to appease the Pope, who disapproved of the marriage between cousins.

The post-war reconstruction of Caen included several parks and gardens, amongst a pleasing mixture of modern and traditional architecture. On the outskirts of the town is the vast Peace Museum (Musée Pour la Paix).

Port Guillaume

Port Guillaume at Dives-sur-Mer six miles to the east of Ouistreham, was inaugurated on 15 June 1991 with the opening of a 600 berth yacht basin. The single gate is open day and night, when there is a depth of 2 m over the sill (approximately 6 to 6½ hours each tide). The channel through the sandbanks can be navigated over this period by craft drawing up to 1.5 m. The first of the red and green channel buoys is 1.5 nm from the yacht basin. The channel is narrow, and at low water can be crossed on foot. Some of the buoys are lit, and there is a shore light for night entry.

There are no shops around the yacht harbour, but it is only about 2 km, over the footbridge across the Dives River, to the busy seaside resort of Cabourg, with its fine beach flanked by bathing tents. There is a casino here, several five-star hotels and many shops and restaurants.

About the same distance to the east is Houlgate, another holiday resort but also a fishing port (the quayside is to port on entering the River Dives). The resort compares well with neighbouring Cabourg, with another splendid beach, a casino and sporting club.

Before the extensive silting, Dives was a large seaport where William the Conqueror, in 1066, assembled his army and ships to invade England. Now it is a walk of about 20 minutes to the centre of the town – worth a visit to see the Village de Guillaume le Conquerant which was an important staging post. There is still the original *hostellerie*, miniature square and courtyard, surrounded by beautifully restored houses, where local artists and craftsmen display their work. *En route* from the yacht basin to Dives is a covered market, dating back to the 14th and 15th centuries. The market takes place on Saturday mornings.

Deauville

The exclusive resort of Deauville, 7 miles NE of Dives, lies on one side of the River Touques, with the fishing harbour and resort of Trouville on the other. Many associate Deauville with its wooden promenade, where one strolled the *planches* to see or be seen. Behind the promenade are large hotels, including the famous Hôtel Normandy, and immaculate lawns. Meticulously straight lines of gaudy umbrellas are planted along the spotlessly clean beach. The short season at Deauville is now extended into September by the international film festival, second only to Cannes. The resort still draws the wealthy to yachting, horse racing, polo, dressage, show jumping, golf, tennis and gambling at what some claim to be the most famous casino in the world.

In spite of these exclusive surroundings, the cost to a boatowner for an overnight stay here is far from prohibitive. There is a choice of two harbours for visiting craft: Port Deauville, a private development, and the Port Municipal. Having passed between the outer breakwaters, Port Deauville is reached through the lock immediately to starboard. Visiting boats berth alongside the first pontoons, again to starboard. Boats using the Municipal Yacht Harbour, carry on to pass between the inner pier heads, making for the basin gate ahead. Once inside, visitors berth alongside each other, off the wall on the far side of the basin. The

There is a 600 berth yacht basin at Port Guillaume on the River Dives.

lifting bridge, giving access to a second basin, may also be open, but the Bassin Morny is for local boats only.

One advantage Port Deauville has over the Municipal Yacht Harbour, is that the lock is operated whenever there is sufficient water to cross the extensive drying sandbanks off the entrance. A boat with a draught of 1.5 m can cross the sandbanks 4½ hours either side of HW at neap tides, and longer at springs. Port Deauville is also nearer the beach and the Promenade des Planches. Built as part of a residential development, with a yacht club for residents only, the immediate facilities for visiting yachts are limited, with a shower block, *crêperie*, bar and small shop selling provisions.

The gate giving access to the Municipal Yacht Harbour remains open for 2 hours either side of HW, when the Bassin Morny lifting bridge will be raised. This means a long walk round the end of the basin to reach the beach. When the lifting bridge is down, it is only a short walk to the elegant Deauville Yacht Club. The Municipal Yacht Harbour is nearer to the town centre and the casino. Although Trouville, connected to

A yacht entering Deauville with Trouville's casino to port.

Deauville by a bridge, does not cater for yachts, it is well worth taking a look at the fishing port, strolling along the promenade, or exploring the maze of narrow streets flanked by old buildings.

Deauville is conveniently close to the Seine estuary, and boats with limited power, locking out of Port Deauville at the first opportunity, can carry the flood all the way round to Honfleur.

Honfleur

With the building of a lock at Honfleur in 1992, this small ancient fishing port took on a new significance for pleasure craft navigating the tidal Seine. In previous years the approach channel dried, and the Vieux Bassin could only be entered around HW. Honfleur was rarely on the itinerary of a Seine cruise, for the tides dictated that most craft plying between Rouen and the sea would be off Honfleur at the end of the ebb or the beginning of the flood. Dredging the approach channel has now made it possible for craft drawing up to 1.5 m to enter or leave Honfleur at any state of the tide. The lock is worked round the clock, opening on the hour for entry, and on the half-hour for departure. These opening times are flexible, as there may well be additional openings for fishing boats or sightseeing *vedettes*.

In practice, if a boat arrives after the half-hour opening for leaving traffic, the outer gates will have been left open, and craft can proceed straight into the lock, instead of staying outside, where there is no convenient place to wait. Once through the lock, boatowners will usually have to wait for an opening of the road bridge (Pont de la Lieutenance) to gain access into the Vieux Bassin. During the season (June to mid-September), there are openings at 0730, 0830, 0930, 1030, 1730, 1830, 1930 and 2030. The only place to wait between the bridge and the lock is clearly signposted (a short section of wall to starboard when entering, close to the bridge). The long wall to starboard is strictly reserved for commercial craft. In practice, craft leaving the basin can usually go straight into the lock.

12

The Vieux Bassin, the popular yacht harbour at Honfleur.

In the Vieux Bassin, the visitors' pontoons are midway along the Quai Sainte-Catherine, which is to starboard on entering. In high season, particularly at weekends, visiting boats are rafted together, sometimes extending half-way across the basin. The last to arrive may have ten fore-decks to clamber over to reach shore. Honfleur does get crowded, both afloat and ashore. Apart from this one reservation, the ancient town with its pastel-coloured buildings reflected in the water, is a delight.

Someone from the local yacht club (Cercle Nautique Honfleur) calls on visiting boats to collect the mooring fees and supply the code to the shower block, which is about five minutes' walk from the pontoons, across the roadbridge to the top end of the fishing harbour. Around the basin are narrow, cobbled streets with leaning houses, where there are many shops, restaurants and art galleries. The square is dominated by the wooden church of St Catherine, which was constructed in the 15th century by local boatbuilders. It is hardly surprising that for years Honfleur has been a mecca for painters, who are nearly always to be found working around the basin. Eugene Boudin was a local artist, and invariably one of the Honfleur galleries will be featuring his work.

················◆················

3 *Passage-making restrictions* • *Maximum boat dimensions* • *Speed restrictions* • *VHF radio* • *Documentation*

Passage-making restrictions

On the tidal Seine, upriver of the giant Pont de Normandie, pleasure craft must not be underway between buoys 27/28 and Rouen over the period between 30 minutes after sunset and 30 minutes before sunrise. Pleasure craft are prohibited from using the Seine in bad visibility.

Maximum boat dimensions

Length and beam: NA (large merchant ships use tidal Seine).

Draught 3.5m.

Height: 6m (to clear Rouen bridges on highest tide with safety margin). More precise calculation is 15.3m less height of tide (see section 4 for details of lowering masts).

Speed restrictions

Commercial and pleasure craft
From the sea to the outskirts of Rouen (PK260[1]): 28 km/h (15 kn).

---

[1] PK (Pointe Kilometrique) is a measurement in kilometres showing, on the Seine, the distance from Paris.

Downriver from the outskirts of Rouen (PK260) to the first of Rouen's bridges (PK242): 14 km/h (7.5 kn).

Pleasure boats over 20 tons
From the first of Rouen's bridges (PK242) to the upriver outskirts of Rouen (PK233): 12 km/h (6.5 kn).

From the upriver outskirts of Rouen (PK233) to the first lock at Bas-de-Poses (PK202): 18 km/h (9.7 kn).

Pleasure boats under 20 tons
From the first of Rouen's bridges (PK242) to the upriver outskirts of Rouen (PK233): 18 km/h (9.7 kn).

From the upriver outskirts of Rouen (PK233) to the first lock at Bas-de-Poses (PK202): 20 km/h (10.8 kn).

VHF radio

VHF radio is compulsory for craft over 20 m, and strongly recommended for all other pleasure craft on the Seine. Boatowners with VHF, starting a passage from the sea to Rouen, should call up on Ch 73 Rouen Port Control (the prominent radar tower just upriver of the entrance channel to Honfleur), to advise them that the vessel is on passage to Rouen, giving an estimated time of arrival, or indicating a planned overnight stop at Caudebec or Duclair. On the outskirts of Rouen, 'Rouen Port' (the harbour master's office) should be advised on Ch 73 of the boat's arrival. Making the passage downriver, Rouen Port and Rouen Port Control should be likewise notified. English is used for ship/shore communication.

Documentation

A boatowner must be able to produce the craft's registration papers (French Customs have stated that a properly registered UK boat will be assumed to have been dealt with by HM Customs and Excise regarding payment of VAT). No permits are required to use the Seine between the sea and Rouen, but upriver of Rouen (the recognised start of the 'Inland Waterway'), a VNF licence is required for the boat, and the owner must have the International Certificate of Competence (ICC) and a copy of the CEVNI rules – the equivalent of the Collision Regulations, but applied to French inland water.

VNF licence

This is required to navigate those French waterways managed by Voies Navigables de France (VNF), which include the Seine above Rouen. VNF, who issue the licence, offer a choice of three periods – 16 consecutive days on their waterways, 30 days, or yearly. The 30-day licence need not be consecutive days, as it applies only to those days actually under- way on the waterway. (The boatowner is responsible for indicating on the licence the number of days used up at any one time.) The licence has to be displayed on the starboard side of the craft, so that it can be inspected from the outside. The charges are based on the dimensions of a boat (overall length × beam), falling into five categories – under 12 sq m, 12–25 sq m, 25–40 sq m, 40–60 sq m and over 60 sq m.

There are VNF offices at Le Havre, Rouen, Conflans-Ste-Honorine and Paris (see below). Details required with payment are: name and address of boatowner, name of boat, home port, overall length and beam, registration number and type of licence required. Sight will also be required of the registration document and International Certificate of Competence (see below).

Postal application to any of the offices listed below is possible, but allow plenty of time. Initially (after 1 April) write to the French Government Tourist Office, 178 Piccadilly, London W1V 0AL, asking for details of the cost of VNF licences to use the French waterways. A postal application should include a cheque payable to the VNF in French francs, with photocopies of the Registration Certificate and ICC, and the type of licence required (state dates if applying for the 16-day licence).

VNF local offices

La Citadelle
Avenue Lucien Corbeaux
76600 Le Havre
Tel: 2 35 22 99 34

71 avenue Jacques Chastellain
76000 Rouen (conveniently
close to Halte Plaisance)
Tel: 2 32 08 31 70

Cours de Chimay
78700 Conflans-Ste-Honorine
Tel: 2 39 72 73 09 (for location
see page 54)

18 quai d'Austerlitz
75013 Paris
Tel: 1 45 84 85 69 (for location
see plan on page 61)

International Certificate of Competence (ICC)

Along with some other European countries, the French authorities now require the owner/skipper to be able to prove competence to navigate the inland waterways. Owners of craft less than 15 m in length and with a top speed under power of less than 20 km/h (10.8 kn), must be able to produce an International Certificate of Competence (ICC). This is issued by the RYA. Those with the RYA Day Skipper (Practical), or more advanced qualifications will be eligible for the ICC without further examination. Others, however experienced, must take an elementary practical test, together with a written/oral examination to qualify for the ICC. The certificate is only issued to UK nationals and UK residents. Those owners of boats more than 15 m or capable of more than 20 km/h, are advised to have the ICC, although at the present time there is no recognised British equivalent to the French certification covering use of such craft on the waterways.

CEVNI regulations

The French authorities also insist that a copy of the regulations (CEVNI) for using the waterways is carried on board. The booklet, *Vagnon Carte de Plaisance*, is recognised as such a document, and is available from the RYA.

RYA booklets

The RYA publish in alternate years (with a supplement between publications) two useful booklets called *Planning a Foreign Cruise*. C1 covers European countries bordering the Atlantic and Baltic, C2 covers countries bordering the Mediterranean and Black Sea. Both contain information on the French inland waterways regulations. They are two of many RYA booklets (two titles are freely available annually to members). For membership, details of ICC and examination centres, and publications (which can be purchased by non-RYA members), apply to: RYA, RYA House, Romsey Road, Eastleigh, Hampshire SO50 9YA. Tel: 01703 627400.

4 Lowering or raising masts

Le Havre

Masts can be lifted out within the Port de Plaisance complex, but there are no storage facilities here for masts and spars. Apply to the Capitainerie at the Port de Plaisance.

Rouen – PK251 – Darse des Docks (see plan on page 88)

Lozai Maintenance, a shipyard on the outskirts of Rouen, will remove, store and raise the mast, and provide the slings. They occupy the Darse des Docks (entrance just downstream of some vast half-dome-shaped grain

Mast being raised in the Darse des Docks, Rouen

silos). The entry to the basin leaves the docks Aval light structure to starboard and Docks Amont to port. A yacht makes for the crane on the end of a jetty extending out from Lozai's buildings. If free, moor alongside the metal pontoon on the river side of the jetty. If there is no space, try the other side, or the end of the jetty. Contact should then be made with the office.

The office hours (Monday to Friday only) are

0715–1145
1315–1630.

It is not necessary to make arrangements in advance with Lozai Maintenance. If arriving after close of business, a yacht can spend the night here, but there are no shops or other facilities within walking distance.

Rouen – PK245 – Bassin St Gervais (*see plan on page 89*)

There is a small, self-operated derrick suitable for lifting out light masts (no more than 7 m) at no charge. The adjacent pontoon is available for a maximum 48-hour stay (about 20 minutes' walk from the docks to the centre of Rouen). There is a total lack of security, so any yacht berthed here should not be left unattended.

Larger masts can be removed in the Bassin St Gervais by Rouen Port Authority, who operate the large cranes along the basin's Quai de l'Ouest. Contact can be made with the harbour master's office on Ch 73, or craft can proceed another 1.6 km upriver and secure alongside the Port Authority pontoon (painted green) – see plan on page 89. The Capitainerie is the nearest tall office block, where arrangements can be made to have the mast lifted out. Paperwork must be completed before a crane operator can be allocated. The Port Authority's charges are considerably more than those of Lozai Maintenance, and there are no storage facilities. The boatowner must have the mast ready for lifting out and provide the slings. The hours during which the crane can usually be operated are 0730–1130 and 1330–1730 Monday to Friday. Requests for the crane must be made during the afternoon for the next morning, and during the morning for the afternoon of the same day. Saturday morning is also a possibility, providing the Capitainerie have been given advance notice (Friday afternoon at the latest).

5 Refuelling

Le Havre

Twenty-four-hour availability (except around LW). The fuelling pontoon is in the SE corner of the first yacht harbour. Pumps are self-operated with credit cards (American Express, Master Card, Visa). Maximum purchase in any 24-hour period is 600 fr.

Between Le Havre and Rouen

There are two possible stopping places at Caudebec-en-Caux (section 10) and Duclair (section 11). Garages are within walking distance of the landing stages at both places.

Rouen

The fuelling pontoon is off Villetard boatyard, just downriver of Municipal Halte Plaisance (see plan on page 89). It is usually necessary to contact the chandlery for the pump attendant. Opening hours are 0900–1130, 1400–1815 (closed Sundays and Mondays).

There is a fuelling barge, *Sargasse*, upriver of the town centre, at Amfreville (PK239) – see plan on page 89. Open 7 days a week.

6 Passage planning from the sea to Rouen:
Le Havre • Honfleur • Rouen

Boats leaving Le Havre's Port de Plaisance stay in the main deepwater channel, between the red and green buoys, until 1.6 nm from the harbour breakwaters at No 11 buoy. From this position it is safe to come round to the south to cross over from one side of the Seine's estuary to the other, keeping well to seaward of the shallows, which are marked with several buoys and a prominent pole. This detour from Le Havre's Port de Plaisance to Ratier NW (the first of the buoys marking the Chenal de Rouen) is about 5 nm.

The distance between Ratier NW and Rouen's Halte Plaisance is 126 km (68 nm).

Many big ships ply between Rouen and the sea.

- Boats underway at the maximum permitted speeds of 28 km/h (15 kn) up to La Bouille (PK260), and 14 km/h (7.5 kn) between La Bouille and the centre of Rouen, can complete the passage from Ratier NW buoy to Rouen in about 4 hours with the flood.
- Boats with an engine capable of 10 kn, again taking the flood, will be underway for about 6 hours.
- Owners of craft with 10 bhp engines, capable of a maximum 5 kn, have to plan the passage carefully, making the optimum use of the tide (which in certain sections can reach 5 kn), and at the same time conforming with the regulations which prohibit pleasure craft from being underway on the tidal Seine between sunset and sunrise (see section 3).

It must be appreciated that, apart from the somewhat exposed landing stages at Caudebec (where there are also some visitors' moorings) and Duclair (sections 10 and 11), there are no other recognised stopovers between the sea and Rouen. The piles to which barges may secure, the huge mooring buoys used by large ships, and the occasional inviting-looking quay, are not for pleasure craft, as they will invariably be in the current and unprotected from the considerable wash of passing traffic. Anchoring in the tidal Seine should only be attempted in an emergency, because of the wash, strong current and poor holding ground.

Boats making 4½ to 5 kn through the water, can complete the passage in about 12 hours from Ratier NW buoy in the estuary (10½ hours starting from Honfleur) if, by careful planning, the tide is carried almost all the way up to Rouen.

The ebb and flow graphs on pages 22–23 illustrate that a boat will have about 10 hours of flood, which starts progressively later upriver.

Position		Flood starts
PK	Place	(based on LW Le Havre)
365	Seaward end of Digue du Ratier	LW + 1 hr 15 mins
344	La Roque	LW + 2 hrs
326	Courval	LW + 3 hrs
318	Vatteville	LW + 3 hrs 15 min
285	Mesnil	LW + 4 hrs 30 min
265	Val des Leux	LW + 5 hrs
242	Halte Plaisance – Rouen	LW + 6 hrs 15 min

The flood at Rouen, starting at LW Le Havre + 6 hrs 15 min, continues until LW + 11 hrs. The ebb in Rouen is rarely more than 1 kn, so reasonable progress will still be made after the tide has turned. Yachts with limited power, stopping off in the outskirts of Rouen to have the mast lifted out, should complete the passage in about 11 hours (9½ hours starting from Honfleur).

Starting times for boats with limited power (10 bhp)	
Le Havre	LW Le Havre – 30 min
Ratier NW	LW Le Havre + 30 min
Honfleur*	LW Le Havre + 2 hrs

* See section 2 for times that the Honfleur lock is worked

The possibilities of a passage between the sea and Rouen on one tide, and in daylight hours, are naturally more likely to occur between May and early August, with the shorter nights. If the time at which the flood starts in the estuary, or off Honfleur, makes it impossible to cover the distance during daylight hours, then consideration must be given to breaking the journey either at Caudebec (PK310), or Duclair (PK278) (see sections 10 and 11).

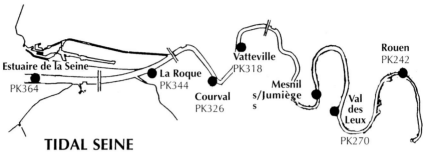

TIDAL SEINE

(Reproduced by kind permission of Port Autonome de Rouen)

Based on hours after LW Le Havre (bottom scales on the graphs), the following seven graphs show the strength of the tide in knots at springs (Coef 90), mid-way (Coef 70) and neaps (Coef 45).

PK (Pointe Kilometrique) denotes position. Refer to same KM number on river plans.

From the graphs it will be seen that at springs around PK326, the flood reaches almost 5 knots.

In Rouen, flood and ebb rarely exceed 2 knots.

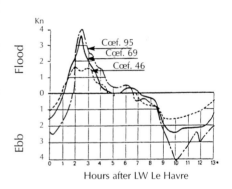

Estuaire de la Seine
PK364

Hours after LW Le Havre

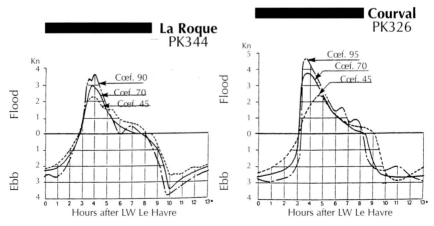

La Roque
PK344

Courval
PK326

Hours after LW Le Havre

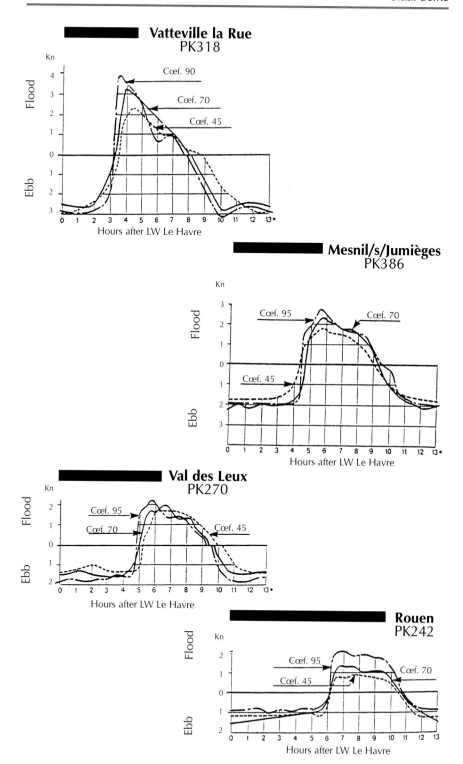

Vatteville la Rue
PK318

Mesnil/s/Jumièges
PK386

Val des Leux
PK270

Rouen
PK242

7 Return passage planning from Rouen to the sea: Rouen • Honfleur • Le Havre

For boats with limited power (maximum 5 kn), the opportunities of completing a daylight passage between Rouen and Honfleur/the sea are restricted to only a few days in the month. The flood starts progressively earlier down river. Interpreting the tidal charts on pages 22–23 correctly is essential. Unlike the upriver passage, boats with limited power will be motoring for several hours with the tide against them:

Position	Ebb starts
Km Place	(based on LW Le Havre)
242 Halte Plaisance – Rouen	LW – 1 hr
	Adverse flood starts (based on LW Le Havre)
265 Val des Leux	LW + 5 hrs
285 Mesnil	LW + 4 hrs 30 min
318 Vatteville	LW + 3 hrs 15 min
326 Courval	LW + 3 hrs
344 La Roque	LW + 2 hrs
365 Seaward end of Digue du Ratier	LW + 1 hr 15 min

At a modest 5 kn, a single passage to the sea can be completed in about 14 hours (Honfleur 12½ hours) provided the adverse flood is met well upriver, avoiding the strong tides downstream of Quillebeuf-sur-Seine (PK332), when a spring flood could bring a boat with limited power to a virtual standstill for several hours.

For boats with limited power (maximum 5 kn) the best time to leave Rouen is at LW Le Havre. The contrary flood will be met after about 5 hours, but should be no more than 2 kn against, leaving sufficient time to complete the passage to Honfleur and the sea on the new ebb. If making for the sea/Le Havre, it is essential that the navigator plots the boat's progress regularly, to make certain that the craft will not get caught by the changing tide between Honfleur and the sea (distance Honfleur to Ratier NW 6.5 nm). Alternatively a stop is possible at Caudebec or Duclair (see sections 10 and 11).

8 Chenal de Rouen • Pont de Normandie • Pont de Tancarville

Chenal de Rouen

The Chenal de Rouen, on the south side of the estuary, which is used by large ships plying between the sea and Rouen, is particularly narrow. On arriving at the beginning of the Chenal de Rouen around LW, the dikes, marked with poles, will be clearly visible. The channel from the Ratier NW buoy to just downriver of the Tancarville bridge (distance 12 nm) is well marked with red and green buoys. Pleasure craft must not enter the channel, keeping just outside the red buoys (see plans on pages 81 and 83). The channel buoys are moored in a minimum 1.7 m.

The woods downriver of Honfleur give a taste of what is to come, but generally the surroundings in the estuary are bleak, with mile after mile of refineries upriver from Le Havre, and vast stretches of marshland beyond.

Pont de Normandie

This impressive bridge, 3 km upriver of Honfleur, was built between 1988 and 1995. With a span of 856 m, suspended by steel stays from two vast 200 m towers, the Pont de Normandie is the largest single-stayed bridge in the world.

Magnificent Pont de Normandie, spanning the Seine estuary.

After the last of the Chenal de Rouen buoys (No 32), pleasure craft continue up the northern side of the river until just before the Tancarville locks and bridge, when upstream pleasure craft cross over to the other side, and stay on this side of the river (passing port to port) until well beyond Rouen.

Pont de Tancarville

This bridge marks the start of the river proper. When it was opened in 1959 it was the longest suspension bridge in Europe, with a span of 600 m, and it is still the longest bridge of this type in France. Prior to 1959 the only means of crossing the Seine below Rouen was by boat.

◆

9 Tancarville canal

Built over 100 years ago, the 25 km Tancarville canal, linking Le Havre with Tancarville, is still used by barges, thereby avoiding the Seine estuary. Pleasure boats are rarely seen on this waterway. Owners of boats, particularly those with a height above the waterline in excess of 7 m, will make only slow progress because of a low bridge which is opened only infrequently by prior arrangement.

For a boat without the 7 m height restriction, the minimum time for making the passage through the docks and along the canal to Tancarville is 4 hours. The distance from Le Havre's Port de Plaisance to Tancarville by sea is 21.5 nm (40 km), but even the slowest boat, at the start of the flood, will cover the sea passage from the pontoons to the bridge in under 5 hours (1–1½ hours from Honfleur), and all river traffic has a considerable advantage over boats using the canal, since the former can choose the best time to start the passage up the Seine, whereas the canal traffic is restricted to lock-operating times.

Reaching the Tancarville canal from Le Havre's yacht harbour involves motoring past the vast tower that houses the port's Capitainerie, and entering the Arrière Port. From here, access to the canal proper is gained through the Bassin Bellot and the Bassin Vétillart, which involves two locks operated HW – ½ to HW + 2 hrs. There are 6 lifting bridges over the canal, but the last one at Le Hode (headroom 7 m) requires 24 hours' notice, and does not open between 1100 and 1700. There may be a wait at some of the other lifting bridges, depending on the time of day and road traffic. Access to the Seine at Tancarville is restricted to the lock working times HW – 4 to HW + 3 hrs 15 min. This is a problem for slower boats wanting to reach Rouen on one tide, as it is difficult to moor outside the lock to await the beginning of the next flood.

Anyone contemplating using the Tancarville canal should consult the Port de Plaisance Capitainerie, who will be able to provide details of the bridge openings and signals required. Downstream traffic (Tancarville to Le Havre) has priority over upstream traffic. There is a speed limit of 10 km/h (5.4 kn). There are no stopping places for pleasure boats, except between the fourth and fifth mobile bridges, where there are quays at the head of the entrance to a short spur, leading to the centre of Harfleur (about 5 minutes' walk). Now in the industrial suburbs of Le Havre, parts of the attractive old quarter of the town still serve as a reminder of the importance of Harfleur centuries ago, when it was one of the main sea ports in the entrance to the Seine.

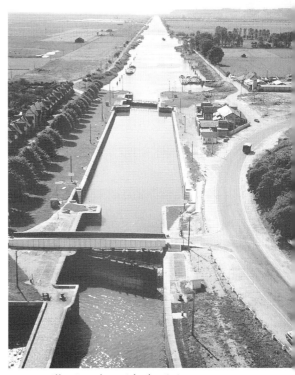

Tancarville Canal avoids the Seine estuary, but is little used by pleasure craft.

10 *Caudebec-en-Caux* • *Pont de Brotonne* • *La Mailleraye-sur-Seine*

After Tancarville, there is extensive marshland, and the huge refinery at Port Jérôme on one side. The high ground behind shows the original path of the Seine, when parts of the estuary were over 7 miles wide with an abundance of sandbanks.

On the other side of the river, five green buoys mark the Banc de Radicatel, followed by four red buoys marking the shallows to port. **Aizier** (PK323), which consists of no more than a few houses, is the limit of the salt water. One hundred years ago, it was possible to cross the river here on foot. It took 120 years of constant dredging to make the tidal Seine navigable by large ships at all states of the tide. Beyond Aizier is the start of the Parc Naturel Regional de Brotonne, which is made up of vast areas of forest, much of which runs right down to the water's edge.

Having entered the river proper, it is essential to keep a good lookout astern, because large, towering freighters can creep up surprisingly unobtrusively. They must be allowed to overtake in the deeper water. The sight of a large ship, closing at 15 kn, can be intimidating, but this should not prompt a rapid alteration of course to hug the river bank as this may take the boat into shallows where there are sometimes unmarked hidden boulders.

Caudebec-en-Caux

On the outskirts of Villequier, the marshland gives way to steep chalk cliffs. Caudebec-en-Caux (PK310), another 4 km upriver, is the first of the two possible stopping places for pleasure craft. There is a substantial landing stage here, which is used by the tourist boats that ply between Honfleur and Paris. In recent years this traffic has declined. The trips are expensive, and the operators have to rely on being fully booked to offset the cost of river pilots on the tidal Seine – obligatory for all craft, irrespective of size, carrying fare-paying passengers. On those occasions when passengers disembark at Caudebec, they are met on the landing stage by someone in traditional costume, bearing gifts of Calvados, a local brandy made from apples. In practice, much of the time, day and night,

The pontoon at Caudebec-en-Caux is one of the two possible stopping places on the tidal Seine between the sea and Rouen.

the landing stage is available (at no cost) to pleasure craft. It is, however, essential to check with the local tourist office at the Hôtel de Ville (5 minutes' walk along the waterfront downstream of the landing stage) or to telephone in advance (Tel: 2 35 95 90 12).

As a stopping place, Caudebec has one distinct advantage over Duclair (PK278). Just a kilometre downstream of the landing stage is the pilot station, where all ships plying between Rouen and the sea change pilots. This means that hereabouts the big ships reduce speed almost to a standstill, so the effect of their wash is minimal. Even so, it is prudent to have several large fenders out, when lying alongside the landing stage. If this is occupied, there are five visitors' buoys just downstream, suitable for craft up to 10 m. They can be uncomfortable, however, as there is no escaping the tide.

The small town of Caudebec attracts many visitors, and has good shopping facilities, banks, restaurants and a nearby garage. Particularly popular is the Musée de la Marine de Seine, which is just beyond the Hôtel de Ville. The three separate buildings are linked by an overhead footbridge. There are many old wooden boats, carefully preserved, housed in the museum, which also has displays of traditional boatbuilding, and many models and plans showing how the Seine has changed over the years. Of particular interest is some old film footage showing the notorious *Mascaret*, the huge tidal wave which used to occur at the equinox, sweeping upstream at the rate of a galloping horse and reaching a height of 3 m off Caudebec, where it was a considerable tourist attraction.

Fortunately for those who cruise the Seine these days, this phenomenon is no more, because the tides in the Seine estuary have been tamed by the dikes off Honfleur. Prior to 1962, hundreds of boats had been wrecked by the *Mascaret*. The dramatic wave also claimed a number of lives, including those of Victor Hugo's daughter, Leopoldine, and her husband Charles Vacquerie. They were drowned at Villequier, 15 minutes' walk downstream of Caudebec, where there is a statue of Victor Hugo staring out across the waters of the river, in which he took a passionate interest, being responsible for much of the planning to dredge the Seine. The Vacquerie family, long associated with pilotage, had a large riverside house at Villequier; this was acquired in 1951 by the Haute Normandie region, and is now the Victor Hugo Museum.

Pont de Brotonne

Just 2 km upriver of Caudebec is the magnificent Pont de Brotonne, built between 1974 and 1977, at that time the largest stayed bridge in the world. With a span of 320 m and a height of 130 m, it is now dwarfed by the similarly constructed Pont de Normandie.

La Mailleraye-sur-Seine

There is talk of a new landing stage at la Mailleraye-sur-Seine (PK304). The small town has a long water frontage, and a temporary visit is possible, but there is no escaping the wash of passing ships or the current. There is a brief change in the scenery in the next section of the Seine, which is industrial for about 4 km, with shallows, marked by buoys, on both sides of the river. It is then back to Normandy farmhouses and châteaux in magnificent countryside, with the Forêt de Brotonne and cliffs to one side and the Abbaye de Jumièges just visible amongst the trees on the other.

11 *Duclair • La Bouille*

Duclair (PK278) is wedged in a gap between the waterside cliffs. There is no mistaking the landing stage (actually a barge), which is 100 yds downstream of the ferry. On the promenade behind the landing stage is a row of flagpoles, carrying the flags of several countries. Conveniently situated across the road from the landing stage is a BP garage and a *boulangerie*, and also many bars and restaurants. Duclair has a large town square, where there are many more shops, including a well-stocked *quincaillerie* (ironmonger), who is also an agent for bottled gas. The prominent large building in the square is the Hôtel de Ville, where the tourist office is located on the ground floor. A visit should be made here to check that the landing stage is free for an extended stay (or telephone in advance: 2 35 05 91 50). Compared with the landing stage at Caudebec, more discomfort will be experienced here from the wash of passing ships. There is also the constant manoeuvring of the adjacent ferry. Secured alongside the barge, a boat must be well protected with several large fenders. With this one qualification, Duclair is a delightful place to visit.

The owner of a vessel coming upstream, and reaching Duclair in the late afternoon or evening, with a mast to be craned out on the outskirts of Rouen, might well consider a stopover at Duclair, instead of spending the night in the industrial surroundings of the docks. Owners of craft with limited power (10 bhp), making the return trip between Rouen and the estuary, may well find Duclair is the place to break the journey, leaving 78 km (42 nm) to cover to Honfleur (see section 7). The mooring buoys, 2 km upstream off the left bank, are private, and do not appear to be as substantial as the public mooring buoys off Caudebec. The long-established yacht club (Cercle Voile Seine-Maritime) is just downstream of the buoys on the Duclair side of the river.

It is possible to land temporarily at **La Bouille** (PK260), which looks

Contact local tourist offices at Duclair (above) and Caudebec to make certain the landing stages are not being used by sight-seeing boats.

delightful from the river, with its backdrop of cliffs and woods. When passing La Bouille, all shipping (including pleasure craft) should report its position and estimated time of arrival to Rouen Port on Ch 73.

······················◆·····················

12 Rouen

Once past La Bouille, the industrial suburbs of Rouen start, with mile after mile of wharfage and large ships on one side, but with cliffs, forest and some large elegant houses on the other. The first of Rouen's basins (Bassin Jupiter) is just beyond a refinery, with a prominent red and white striped chimney. For yachts requiring their masts to be removed (see section 4), the Darse des Docks is another 2 km, with a narrow entrance just before four prominent half-domed-shaped grey silos. Boats can aim straight for the crane, avoiding straying over to the far side of the basin, where it is shallow. The first basin on the other side of the river (Bassin St Gervais, PK245), is the alternative location for having the mast removed by the Port Autonome de Rouen. Boats unable to proceed under the first of Rouen's bridges (7.2–10.8 m headroom), will find a convenient pontoon here, where pleasure craft can stay for a maximum of

31

48 hours. It is only about 15 minutes' walk from the basin into the centre of Rouen, and 5 minutes' walk to the Port's Capitainerie (the large building behind the green Port Authority landing stage), but, because of the dockland locality, a boat should not be left unattended alongside the visitors' pontoon.

The run-in to the centre of Rouen is impressive, with the whole city dominated by the cathedral. Having passed beneath three bridges, pleasure craft take the spur to port, where, just beyond the fourth bridge, the pontoons of the city's Halte Plaisance on the Île Lacroix can be seen. The strength of the current running past the pontoons at certain times may not be fully appreciated, and all craft must be manoeuvred to approach the pontoons against the current.

The Municipal Halte Plaisance, administered by the local Chambre de Commerce, is conveniently close to the centre of Rouen (20 minutes' walk, crossing the Pont Corneille – see plan on page 89). Water and electricity are available on the pontoons, and a separate shower block is accessible at all times. Being an island, the pontoon berths are reasonably peaceful, with no disturbance from road traffic or the wash of barges, which pass the other side of the island. Outside the entry gate to the

The pontoons of the municipal yacht harbour at Rouen, situated on an island, are fairly peaceful and little affected by the wash from river traffic.

Capitainerie and pontoons are a grocer, small supermarket, *boucherie*, launderette and *tabac*/bar. There is also a public telephone. Just downstream of the Halte Plaisance is the fuelling pontoon run by Villetard, who also have a large showroom here, packed with equipment, primarily for motor boats. (For opening hours of the fuelling pontoon see section 5.)

For years, Rouen was a major importer of grain from all over the world, and, although this trade has now declined, the port still ranks as the fourth most important in France. A centre for trade and industry, the offices of the Seine-Maritime Département are located here, along with those of the Conseil Général for the region of Haute-Normandie.

Called the 'City of a Hundred Spires', many of Rouen's historic buildings survived the last war. There are references everywhere to Jeanne d'Arc, who was burnt at the stake by the English in La Place du Vieux-Marché, where there are now some remarkable modern buildings housing an excellent covered market. Making for the Place du Vieux-Marché from the cathedral, visitors walk the length of the narrow, cobbled Rue du Gros-Horloge. This pedestrian way is flanked by half-timbered houses, with many shops, restaurants and bars at ground level. Spanning the street is the Gros-Horloge, a vast clock with an ornately decorated face on each side of the 14th century tower. The bars and restaurants in this old quarter of Rouen are packed with customers until late at night. After dark, the city lights, including the floodlit cathedral, are a superb sight.

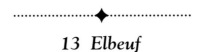

13 Elbeuf

Craft with limited power, leaving Rouen and proceeding upstream, have to calculate the best time to carry the tide to the first lock above Elbeuf. The distance between the Halte Plaisance and the Écluses d'Amfreville is 40 km (21.6 nm). The departure time from Rouen should allow a good safety margin for reaching the lock before it closes at 1900.

The factories on the outskirts of Rouen are soon left behind, as one travels back into the countryside. The only town between Rouen and the Amfreville lock is Elbeuf, where it is possible to moor up alongside the town quay, between the bridges. In doing so, mooring lines must make allowance for the rise and fall of the tide (about 3.5 m) and it is important to remember that there is no escaping the current. One might think that this would be a quiet place to spend the night, but this may not be so, because barges still motor by during the night, no doubt having arranged to pass through the Amfreville lock outside normal hours; they can produce an alarming wash, necessitating some rapid fending off at the town quay.

Just beyond Elbeuf's second bridge, there is the first of the numerous river traffic crossover points between Elbeuf and Paris. These points, clearly shown on the river plans (see pages 90–103), indicate where the river traffic crosses over from one side of the river to the other. Although there are signs on the river bank showing this, they can easily be missed because are obscured by foliage. Years ago, there were none of these crossover points, but the skippers of barges, anxious to save time, would keep to the inside of a long curve in the Seine, and display a blue flag from the wheelhouse, indicating they would not be passing on-coming traffic port-to-port.

In Elbeuf, having passed port-to-port all the way up the Seine from the sea, all shipping (including pleasure craft), must move over to the other bank to pass starboard-to-starboard (see plan on page 90). A craft continues until 2 km beyond the large bridge carrying the A13 motorway, when there is another crossover point, and all upstream traffic moves back to the starboard side of the river. Yet another crossover point comes up just past the factory (PK206), and this is maintained until the Amfreville lock at Le Bas-de-Poses (see sections 15 and 18).

PART II
Non-tidal Seine

between the first lock at Bas-de-Poses
and Paris

14 Navigation • Maximum boat dimensions • Speed restrictions

Navigation

It is essential to follow the river plans (pages 81–103) in order to identify the crossover points (see section 13). It is not sufficient to rely on spotting the crossover signs on the bank, as these are easily missed.

The river plans are designed to show which side of the river craft should be on all sections of the waterway. The dark grey route is followed from Paris to the sea, and the medium grey route from the sea to Paris. All depths in medium and dark grey are safe. The light grey sections mark shallows which should be avoided if no depth is shown, or if the depth indicated is insufficient. The numbers after towns, moorings, locks etc refer the reader to further information included in the text.

At each end of most of the islands, there is an arrow indicating which side to pass to remain in deep water. Anyone ignoring these signs to explore the backwaters behind these islands should check the river plans to make certain that there is sufficient water.

Boatowners should be aware that on most of the bridges there are signs showing which arch to take (see page 105), and also remember that the ferry (bac) crossing points should be approached with caution. In addition, in parts of the river, there are signs indicating that all craft should keep a certain distance from the river bank, where there may well be unmarked shallows. Caution should always be exercised when closing the river bank if there is no clear indication of the depth. Sometimes barges will overtake too close for comfort, but helmsmen must resist the temptation to alter course and perhaps enter shallows.

There is always some current running downstream, but in summer this rarely exceeds 1 km/h (0.5 kn). *One final word of caution: the one-way traffic system in the centre of Paris must be strictly observed.*

Maximum boat dimensions

Height 6 m; draught 3 m; beam 11.4 m.
Above Rouen, on the non-tidal Seine, the only restrictions for most pleasure craft are headroom and draught. The headroom figure is based on the average height of the river – the headroom is occasionally less in the winter, if flooding has raised the river's level. The locks have chambers large enough to accommodate a single shunting barge, pushing along two strings each of four barges.

One of the main attractions of a Seine cruise is exploring the backwaters.

Between Rouen and central Paris: The maximum permitted draught (*tirant d'eau*) is 3 m.

Speed restrictions

Speed restrictions on the River Seine (excluding backwaters etc) are as follows:

Pleasure boats over 20 tons
Upriver outskirts of Rouen (PK233) to outskirts of Paris (PK9): 18 km/h (9.8 kn).

Central Paris: 12 km/h (6.5 kn).

Pleasure boats under 20 tons
Upriver outskirts of Rouen (PK233) to Paris (including central Paris): 20 km/h (10.8 kn).

All pleasure craft
Seine backwaters, or 20 m off moored boats, pontoons etc: 12 km/h (6.5 kn) or as indicated by the speed restriction signs (see page 104).

✦

15 Locks

With the decline in commercial traffic, the lock-keepers undertake to limit the waiting time for pleasure craft to no more than 30 minutes. This is very different to the situation years ago, when making the passage between Rouen and Paris could involve a wait of an hour or two outside some of the locks, in long queues of barges, until the lock-keeper decided to squeeze in a pleasure boat, right at the back of the lock.

Approaching a lock

VHF is not obligatory for craft under 20m, but being able to communicate with the lock-keepers can save time, and sometimes gain access, if a boat is approaching outside normal working hours. For a yacht which has had the mast removed at Rouen, and lost the use of the mast-top VHF aerial, there is something to be said for a temporary aerial, which can lie on the deck and still be more than adequate for communicating at close range. To avoid interference, the channel used by the lock-keepers is either 22 or 18 (see box on page 41).

The normal routine is to let the lock-keeper know when the vessel is perhaps 10 minutes away, and indicate whether it is on passage upstream (*montant*) or downstream (*avalant*). Those who might be a little shy of using their limited French vocabulary, could, for the first few times, write down beforehand what they wish to say, eg '*Écluse d'Andresy* (repeat) *Ici yacht 'Bluebell' montant* (repeat). *J'arrive en ... minutes.*' It may be necessary to wait some time for a reply, and until one gets used to the terminology, the reply may not be immediately understood. Generally, the lock-keeper will acknowledge, and indicate either that the yacht can continue straight into the lock (and sometimes indicate which chamber), or that he is preparing the lock, or that there may be a wait.

Entry is authorised by traffic lights (red: no entry, red and green: standby, and green: enter). Where the lights are displayed indicates which chamber is being prepared. Sometimes, particularly when viewed against the sun, it can be impossible to make out which lights are switched on, making it necessary to circle close to the lock to read the lights.

Mooring

Once inside the lock, it is essential to moor to the bollards beside the lock. There will be no one to help with the lines, with the only surveillance being that of the lock-keeper, perched up above in his control tower. When passage-making upstream, some skippers, even with several crew aboard, try to avoid sending one of them up a grimy ladder with head and stern ropes. Instead, the crew attempt to hang on to the ladder with a boat hook. This should be avoided, as there can be some turbulence, particularly if forced to the front of the lock. If the lock is shared with a barge, there will be more turbulence as the barge motors out.

Pleasure boats should never attempt to moor up alongside a barge. Even with only two people on board, locking-in presents no problem, if one of the crew is reasonably agile. While one person hangs on temporarily to a ladder, the other climbs ashore with head and stern ropes (a bowline over each shoulder leaves the hands free). These can then be dropped over the bollards, and then the crew rejoins the boat. In practice, the lock-keeper allows a crew plenty of time to climb ashore and moor up.

Descending is much easier, with no turbulence as the sluices are

Barges have priority over all pleasure craft, but it is unusual to have to wait for more than 30 minutes to enter any of the Seine's locks.

opened up, and by doubling up, the ropes can be released from the deck. The bollards are placed for the use of barges, so they can be some distance from the bow and stern of a pleasure boat. At the last lock coming downstream from Paris, the length of the lines might have to be 25–30 m, so that they can be doubled back from the bollards, to cope with an exceptional LW range at Amfreville. *It is strictly forbidden to tow tenders through a lock.*

A stout plank secured outside the fenders is useful, as there are recesses along the walls of some of the locks.

Operating times

The locks are operated between 0700 and 1900, and over this period there is no charge to pleasure craft. Outside these hours passage through a lock is possible by prior arrangement, and on payment of a modest charge. Although the barge traffic is much reduced these days, the traffic does continue after 1900, and if a barge skipper has made arrangements to use the lock outside normal hours, the lock-keeper will invariably let the pleasure craft through, free of charge, at the same time. If a boat is just going to fail to reach a lock by 1900, and her owner is pressed for time, a barge steaming up astern may provide the opportunity of passing through the lock, and perhaps motoring on for another three or four hours. It is always worth checking the traffic situation by VHF with the lock-keeper to find out if he is staying on after 1900. The locks are worked 7 days a week, with the exception of certain public holidays. Printed information, and sometimes the advice at a yacht harbour Capitainerie, may indicate that a lock is closed on a particular day, for example, 8 May. In practice, a telephone call to the lock-keeper may establish that there will be an opening at a certain time (for which there will be a nominal charge).

French public holidays are as follows: 1 January, Easter Sunday, Whit Sunday, 1 May, 8 May, 25 May, 5 June, 14 July, 15 August, 1 November, 11 November and 25 December.

The seven locks between Rouen and Paris are listed below, along with the rise/drop inside the lock, the VHF channel used to contact the lock-keeper, and the distance in km from the centre of Paris.

Locks between Rouen and Paris			
	Range (m)	VHF	Km to Paris
Amfreville	4.40–7.90*	Ch 18	202
Notre Dame de la Garenne	4.02	Ch 22	161
Méricourt	5.13	Ch 18	121
Andrésy	2.84	Ch 22	73
Bougival	3.25	Ch 22	49
or			
Chatou	3.25	Ch 18	45
Suresnes	3.17	Ch 22	17
*HW–LW			

Most pleasure craft tend to use Bougival instead of Chatou. Bougival has an Halte de Plaisance (see section 16), and the town facilities are within a few minutes' walk. There are three chambers in use at Bougival, compared with one at Chatou (where there is more water for loaded barges), so there may be a longer wait at Chatou. In terms of distance, there is nothing to choose between them.

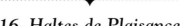

16 *Haltes de Plaisance*

Six public pontoons are freely available to craft on passage between Mantes-la-Jolie and Paris. Some have water and electricity. The maximum stay is 48 hours. Early cruising vessels (May and June) may well have a pontoon to themselves. Each Halte de Plaisance is listed below, identified by the nearest town/village with an indication of which side of

Haltes de Plaisance		
Location	Bank	Km to Paris
Limay	backwater R	109
Meulan	backwater R	93
Andresy	backwater R	73
La Frette	R	63
Bougival	upstream of lock R	48
Chatou	R	45

the river the pontoon is positioned (coming down the Seine, they are all on the right-hand side) and the distance in km from the centre of Paris.

Limay The centre of the small town is 10 minutes' walk from the pontoon. Alternatively, one may cross bridges to the other side of the Seine, to the large old town of Mantes-la-Jolie.

Meulan Perhaps the top-rated *halte* for location, being beside parkland and close to shops. There is an excellent market near the pontoon, on Monday and Friday mornings.

Andrésy Close to the lock. One or two shops and a supermarket are reasonably close, but some way from the centre of town.

Meulan, one of six Haltes de Plaisance for which there is no charge, but the maximum stay is 48 hours.

La Frette Located on the main river. There are no nearby shops, and it is a long climb to the centre of the town.

Bougival Close to the lock, although sometimes wedged between barges. It is a short walk across the bridge to the town centre, which has all the necessary facilities. There is a market on Wednesday and Saturday mornings.

Chatou This is only accessible if taking the Bougival arm of the Seine. La Maison Fournaise (for the restaurant/museum, see section 23) is just upstream of the bridge. The centre of Chatou is across the bridge, but some distance from the pontoon.

17 Refuelling

In the non-tidal Seine between Rouen and Paris there are plenty of stopping places, with a garage within walking distance, to fill jerry cans.
   Alongside fuelling facilities are available at:

Rolleboise (PK119 – see plan on page 96). Open 0700–1900.

Conflans-Ste-Honorine (PK70 – see plan on page 98). There are several fuelling barges between the bridges. Only the Mobil barge, *Defiance*, can be used by pleasure craft. Contact should be made on VHF Ch 10, to make certain it is convenient to berth alongside. Open daily 0700–1200 and 1300–2000.

Paris (PK4 – see plan on page 102). The Touring Club de France has provided a fuelling pontoon for pleasure boats between the Pont des Invalides and Pont Alexandre III. Open daily 0900–1700.

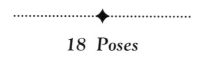

18 Poses

Having successfully negotiated the first of the Seine locks, you might consider stopping off for a couple of hours or staying nearby overnight. Coming back down the Seine, this last section of non-tidal river is a good place to stop for the night if arriving at the lock after closing time, when the crew can enjoy the surroundings, and then be ready to pass through the lock at the first opportunity the next day. There are berths alongside, just upriver of the lock, or a yacht can moor in the chamber just outside the wall of the lock. The nearby bar-restaurant, Les Écluses, is a lively place, with music and dancing on some afternoons. It is open during the day on Monday and Wednesday to Sunday, and in the evenings on Friday, Saturday and Sunday (also Wednesday and Thursday in July and August).

There are narrow channels between the islands 1 km upriver of the lock. These cuts lead into a backwater, and an alternative stopping place at Poses. Make for the mooring alongside the river bank, 100 m upriver of La Louvière Auberge, with its covered platform extending into the river (see plan on page 91). The tranquil surroundings, alongside at Poses, provide a taste of what is to come, when a boat leaves the main river to explore behind one of the Seine's many islands. There is a delightful walk upriver, along the towpath. The only shop conveniently close is a *boulangerie* (take one of the cuts between the river and the road, and then turn left).

After the Amfreville lock, the cruise takes on a different aspect, without the constraints of the tide, and with a varied choice of places to stop, ranging from sleepy backwaters to well-established yacht harbours. To sample these backwaters, leave Poses and continue upriver, behind the islands until PK199, and then slip across the Seine to enter a narrower, more overgrown backwater (minimum depth for the 4 km length is 1.8 m). Avoid the spur off to the right, as there are some submerged trees here. At PK196, still behind the islands, look out for the magnificent 19th century manor house and water-mill, in its own backwater. Le Moulin de Connelles is now a 4-star hotel with a *restaurant gastronomique*, set in seven acres of gardens, which include tennis courts and a swimming pool.

For crews intending to dine here, the boat should enter the backwater upriver of the Moulin de Connelles, where there is usually about 2 m of water, with 1.7 m alongside the private landing stage. Craft of 10m or more can be accommodated, but a phone call (02 32 59 53 33) is recommended to make certain there is room alongside. Alternatively, a yacht can anchor in the downstream approaches to the backwater, and land in the tender on a small private landing stage.

Continuing this exploration behind the islands, at PK193 (minimum depth 2.4 m), there is another old half-timbered water-mill, again in its own shallow backwater. The Moulin d'Andé, which dates back to the end of the 12th century, is a Centre Culturel et Artistique. It is an established meeting place for artists and musicians, with a comprehensive programme of evening classical concerts (1530 most Sundays). Anyone looking for a truly remarkable experience, should contact a tourist office within the region, which will be able to supply dates and details of the concerts (or make contact direct on 2 32 59 90 89). The custom-built theatre and *orangerie*, seating over 100 people and located on the high ground above the mill, is a 10-minute climb up the illuminated terraces. Top international artists are attracted to the Moulin d'Andé, but the cost of a concert visit here is not excessive. There is also an all-inclusive price

A tranquil stretch of river at Poses, the first stopping place on the non-tidal Seine.

covering a pre-concert aperitif at 1930, the concert at 2000, and a buffet supper in the *orangerie* or outside in the gardens at around 2200. Visiting the Moulin d'Andé by boat involves anchoring off the entrance to the mill's backwater, and then going ashore in the tender, landing on the small pontoon provided.

Opposite the village of Muids (PK184) is a narrow cut, spanned by a small bridge, giving access to a large lake that was created by flooding sandpits. There is a harbour here, but it is primarily for small motorboats, and the surroundings are particularly bleak. On the other side of the river at Muids is what looks like a useful pontoon, but this is actually a bathing raft, and part of an area devoted to swimming, complete with a row of changing cubicles and an artificial beach. A pontoon, with a launching ramp, at PK180 is a possible stopping place (1.5 m alongside). This is administered by the nearby camp site.

◆

19 Les Andelys

Just 2 km downriver of Les Andelys is a tiny yacht harbour at Val St Martin (PK176), with 1.5 m in the narrow entrance. There is only one berth for a visiting boat alongside the 15 m quay, immediately to port on entering. There is a nominal charge for an overnight stay, irrespective of the length of the vessel. Water and electricity are on the berth. Showers and provisions are available from the adjoining camp site. There is a boat repair business here, and the proprietor, who lives in the house opposite the road entrance to the camp site, has a limited stock of chandlery. Val St Martin is no more than a tiny hamlet, but this includes Le Manoir de Clairval, a large restaurant overlooking the yacht harbour.

Les Andelys (PK174) has a yacht harbour that was dredged in 1996, which restored this one-time favourite stopping place to something of its former glory. In the preceding years, silting had resulted in many of the local boats moving away, and the place had become somewhat neglected. Administered from the Mayor's office, pontoon space (1.2 m) is provided for visitors, and there are plans to reopen the Capitainerie, which also houses the shower block. (Alternatively, if closed, crews of visiting boats can use the showers on the adjacent camp site.)

The picturesque yacht harbour at Les Andelys.

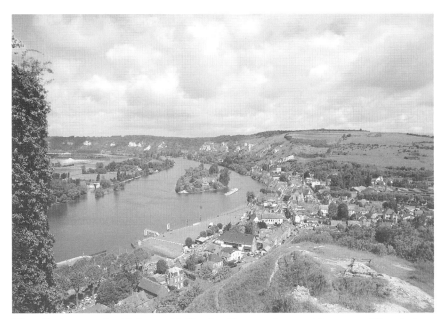

The climb up to the Château Gaillard will reward you with a magnificent view of the Seine below.

The setting is a delight, dominated by the ruins of the Château Gaillard, on the hillside above. Les Andelys is a community made up of Grand Andely, which dates back to the Romans, and Petit Andely, which was a fishing village. Many buildings date back to the 12th century, when Richard Cœur de Lion, King of England and Duke of Normandy, built Château Gaillard as a huge fortress dominating the Seine valley.

Petit Andely is close to the yacht harbour and has a large selection of shops and restaurants, including the 3-star La Chaine d'Or. Those wanting to make the climb up to the Château Gaillard for a magnificent view of the Seine below, should start from the Tourist Office (at the yacht harbour end of the town), following the sign for walkers. There is an open-air swimming pool close to the yacht harbour, which opens daily May to August. In July and August, Monday to Saturday, the hours are: 1000–1230, 1400–1630 and 1715–2000; Sundays: 1000–1230, 1430–1900.

Those who have developed a taste for leisurely cruising, and continuing to explore the backwaters, might consider the cul-de-sac at PK171 (minimum depth 3.5 m). This is navigable for about 1 km, passing the village of Tosny, which is a good place to let go the anchor, in the middle of the river, for a lunchtime stop. Alternatively, leave to starboard the sign marking the end of a submerged dyke extending 400 m upriver from the island, and try another attractive backwater (3.1 m). (See page 93.)

❖

20 Vernon • Giverny

Having passed through the Écluse de Notre-Dame-de-la-Garenne (see section 15), there is little incentive for dawdling, as only another 12 km upstream there is perhaps the most favoured of the Seine's yacht harbours. **Vernon** (PK150) lies in a particularly attractive stretch of the Seine, dotted with wooded islands, and bordered by now familiar cliffs and forest. The visitors' and sailing club pontoons are on the other side of the river at Vernonnet, which is a suburb of Vernon. Caution must be exercised when making for the pontoons, avoiding the covered shoal marked by a pole (see plan on page 94). Approaching from downstream, alter course for the white hut with flagpole (used by the yacht club for starting/finishing races), when it bears approximately 100°T, with the granary astern. This course takes a boat midway between a small island to port and the post to starboard. From upstream, having just passed under Vernon's bridge, head for the hut on a course of approximately N, with the church astern. This cuts between the small island that extends from the base of the bridge to starboard, and the post to port. Boats drawing 1.5 m should continue with caution, heading for the pontoon alongside the hut. If occupied, it can be prudent to moor up alongside a visiting boat to investigate, for there may be insufficient water elsewhere on the pontoon.

Visitors will find themselves in a most delightful setting in the extensive grounds of a manor house, now used as a children's activity centre, where the youngsters take to the water in Optimists and canoes. The washroom/showers used by the centre, and available to visiting crews, are in the adjacent half-timbered building that was originally the stables and accommodation for the servants. Standing in the grounds, overlooking the moorings, are the remains of the Château des Tourelles, and of the much-photographed 12th century bridge and mill. Boat crews receive a friendly welcome from the General Secretary of the Vernon yacht club. The cost of an overnight stay is remarkably good value, and may include a 50 per cent discount for stopping off for another night at Vernon on the homeward trip.

Vernon is a large town, with excellent shopping facilities. Close to the pontoons at Vernonnet are a small grocer, *tabac*/bar, supermarket, restaurant and garage. A stroll across the bridge into the town is recommended. The old quarter, with narrow streets and leaning timbered houses, is situated around the fine 12th century collegiate church of Notre-Dame. Restaurants and bars abound, some with fine views across the water. There is an open-air swimming pool, signposted to the left at the Vernon end of the bridge (the pool is open until 1815).

A friendly welcome is assured at Vernon's yacht club. There is a visitors' pontoon.

Another attraction of Vernon is that **Giverny**, and its beautiful gardens, is only 4 km away. Anyone who is interested in the Impressionist painters should make the pilgrimage, either by taxi, bus or foot, to the village where Claude Monet lived, from 1883 to his death in 1926. Buses leave infrequently from the railway station at Vernon (the times are displayed in the booking hall); a taxi from the pontoons takes about 10 minutes, and arrangements can usually be made with the driver for the return trip. Alternatively, the unremarkable walk takes about 50 minutes, and the main road can be avoided by walking along what used to be a railway track. There is much to see at Giverny, which attracts thousands of visitors. Particularly popular are the gardens created by Monet, and made famous by his paintings of the waterlilies and the Japanese bridge. Inevitably, there is a huge shop, marketing a vast array of goods associated with Monet and Giverny. You can pay to see the gardens on their own, or purchase a ticket for entry to both the gardens and the house.

Young American art students, living in Paris more than 100 years ago, visited this village, and stayed briefly at the local café, run by a Madame Baudry. They returned regularly and, with Claude Monet just up the road, Giverny soon became an artists' colony, centred around what had now become the Hôtel Baudry, with its own studios. Visitors to this modest inn included Renoir, Sisley, Rodin, Pissarro and Clemenceau. Faithfully preserved, the Hôtel Baudry and its attractive gardens are open to the public. The works of several of the expatriate American Impressionists are on display here in the Musée Américain – a huge modern gallery opened in 1992. All three centres are closed to the public on Mondays.

Another 10 km upstream of Vernon and Giverny, is Grande Île, which lies between Bonnières-sur-Seine and the village of Bennecourt. It was on Grande Île that Monet set up his easel, to capture this small backwater on canvas. The artist spent the summer of 1868 staying at the village inn with his young wife. It is still possible to navigate part of this backwater, fetching up at Port St Nicolas, which is Bennecourt's small yacht harbour. Mostly occupied by small motorboats, anything over 8 m long would look somewhat out of place here, but there is certainly space for something larger on the outside of the pontoons. The least depth (1.4 m) is in the entrance to the backwater. Approaching from downstream, continue on well past the entrance, before turning to avoid the shallows off the end of the island (see plan on page 95). The backwater downriver of the yacht harbour is blocked with sunken trees. There is a *boulangerie* here, and, overlooking Port St Nicolas, the Auberge Rendez-vous des Pêcheurs, with a waterside garden. The restaurant is closed on Tuesday and Thursday evenings.

The river between Bonnières-sur-Seine and Vétheuil is particularly lovely, with the Forêt de Moisson on one side and great cliffs on the other, particularly around La Roche Guyon, where remarkable caves and doorways, cut into the chalk, can be clearly seen.

Monet's house and gardens at Giverny, within easy reach of Vernon.

Before moving to Giverny, Claude Monet had rented a large house at Vétheuil (PK128) for three years, during which time he became increasingly absorbed in painting the Seine, making considerable use of a skiff he had designed, incorporating a covered studio. Moored below the house, the skiff was used extensively to explore the local backwaters and islands.

············◆············

21 Port de l'Ilon • Limay

Just upriver of the Méricourt lock (PK121, see section 15) is **Port de l'Ilon.** Invisible from the river, the Port de Plaisance is reached through a cut on the weir side of the river. Around what was a vast area of sandpits, there is a complete range of boatyard facilities, including a travel lift, 12.5 T crane, launching ramps, engineering workshop, yacht brokerage, chandlery, electronics and a long-established boatbuilding business. It is very much in the wilds; extensive landscaping has created attractive wooded surroundings. Showers are available at the Capitainerie. There are a few shops in the village of Guernes (1.8 km). Fuel is available on the other side of the river at Rolleboise (see section 17). Port de l'Ilon can be a useful stopping place if underway downstream after 1900; an early start and passage through the lock can then be achieved the next day.

Just 11 km upriver from the Méricourt lock is **Mantes-la-Jolie** (PK110), and, of more significance to boatowners, the first of the Seine's public Haltes de Plaisance (see section 16), at **Limay**. These are no more than a pontoon with access to the shore, with a water supply and sometimes electricity.

The Halte de Plaisance at Limay is reached by taking the backwater at PK112 (minimum 5.3 m), or those who are more adventurous and who have a boat of the right dimensions can take the very narrow cut (1.5 m) spanned by a low bridge (headroom 2.5 m) at PK110. If there are too many boats alongside the Halte de Plaisance, in the backwater, close to the cut, there are private pontoon berths on both sides where there may be a free mooring.

Limay is a small, quiet town (10 minutes' walk to the centre) and almost a suburb of Mantes-la-Jolie, which is a short walk from the pontoon over the bridge. In spite of some industry, and having suffered considerable bomb damage during World War Two, Mantes-la-Jolie still has some attractive old buildings, including Notre-Dame, which is a fine example of a Gothic collegiate church.

◆

22 Meulan

Leaving the Halte de Plaisance, a boat can continue along the backwater, passing through the remains of the old Limay bridge. Emerging back into the Seine, there are shallows around the end of the island and off the entrance to a large basin, but these are well marked with red and green buoys (see plan on page 96). The next 12 km are industrial, including the vast electricity generating station at Porcheville and one of Renault's factories at Elisabethville. If making for the Halte de Plaisance at Meulan (see section 16), or the restaurant on Belle Île, leave the river at PK99, taking the 6 km backwater (depth 3 m), to Meulan. Alternatively, leave the river just upriver of the bridge at Les Mureaux, taking the narrow cut (depth 2.2 m), passing beneath three sections of bridge and, as the boat comes round to starboard, the Halte de Plaisance will be seen off the grassy bank on the Meulan side of the backwater.

Of the six Haltes de Plaisance, the pontoon at Meulan is perhaps the best for surroundings, being moored off parkland. Meulan is a small town, with all the usual services, but if a boat is at Meulan on a Monday or Friday morning, there is also a splendid market here. Just downriver of the Halte de Plaisance, beyond the bridge, is a pontoon exclusively for those boat crews wishing to dine at the 4-star hotel-restaurant, Mercure.

With Paris less than 100 km by river, and only 40 km by road, there are now more signs of water-sports on the river, evidenced by the two prosperous sailing clubs above Les Mureaux, on the left bank, each with dining rooms overlooking the river, and keeled racing yachts neatly drawn up out of the water. On the same side is the vast complex of the Arienne Space Centre, with its own sailing clubs. The flags of 12 nations fly beside the centre, with one noticeable absentee – the Union Jack.

At Port Maron (PK88) there are a slipway, a travel-lift and private pontoons. Opposite Médan (PK83), on the Île de Médan, is an enormous open-air swimming pool, with small ferries operating a shuttle service between Médan and the island. There are more waterside bars and restaurants, no doubt attracting visitors from the capital.

Port St Louis (PK81), is a yacht harbour accommodating large motorboats. This flooded gravel pit is in bleak surroundings, but there is a full range of services here (apart from fuel). The next two islands, upriver of the Île de Médan, are dotted with elegant houses, with beautiful lawns running down to the water, where there will invariably be a davit and a fast motorboat. Although the backwater between the Île des Mignaux and the town of Poissy is a dead-end, it is an interesting stretch of river to explore. The minimum depth (2.6 m) is in the narrow entrance, between the Poissy end of the island and the remains of an old bridge with a yellow buoy off the end. This backwater is only navigable for 1 km, and then there are shallows. There are many yachts on pontoons, a large swimming pool, a boatyard and a restaurant just before the second bridge.

···················◆····················

23 Andrésy • Conflans-Sainte-Honorine • Bougival • Chatou

Andrésy

There is another Halte de Plaisance (see section 16) upriver of the lock (section 15) at Andrésy (PK73). On passage upriver, to reach the Halte de Plaisance, it is necessary to round the end of the island to port and double back down the backwater. Andrésy is a useful overnight stopping place when passage-making downriver in the evening and planning an early start to pass through the lock the following morning. The Halte de Plaisance is in a quiet part of Andrésy, with shops about 10 minutes' walk from the pontoon. The backwater downstream of the pontoon is navigable (minimum depth 3.6 m) as far as the spur leading off to port where a buoy marks the entrance to the old weir. It is an attractive 2 km stretch between the pontoon and weir, but beware of the many boats on the water from the local rowing club. The coxless fours approach at an alarming speed, oblivious of anything else on the water. The old disused lock is another 1 km further along the shallowing backwater.

53

Conflans-Sainte-Honorine

Upriver of the Andrésy lock and Halte de Plaisance is Conflans-Sainte-Honorine (PK70). The 'Conflans' relates to the convergence of two rivers – the Seine and the Oise. Sainte Honorine is the adopted saint of the bargees, whose craft are moored up here in great numbers. Years ago, Conflans-Sainte-Honorine was bustling with activity on the water, handling annually thousands of working barges. Today, most of these craft are parked ten deep, along the full length of the town quay. Although they are no longer working, they still provide homes, and a chapel, for this colony of bargees.

Conflans-Sainte-Honorine is a good stopping place to take on fuel, with one particular barge on the left bank offering a fuelling service to pleasure craft (see section 17). (Traditionally, the left or right bank assumes a vessel is travelling downstream.) There is a landing stage off the town quay on the right bank, but this is for the exclusive use of the passenger boats. There may be some room on the town quay for a short stay, and any boatowner who has not managed to obtain a river licence for the extent of the cruise will find a VNF office in Cours de Chimay, which is at the downstream end of the town, where the Oise meets the Seine.

Although the sight of factories and office developments is becoming more frequent, there are still stretches of the river in pleasing countryside, passing through waterside villages with elegant houses. There are sailing clubs, and others catering for water-skiers,with more activity on the water, both pleasure and commercial.

The huge barge colony at Conflans-Ste-Honorine.

Bougival and Chatou

Bougival (PK48) is a large town. There is a choice of two Haltes de Plaisance in the vicinity, either of which can be a useful place to stop off, prior to entering Paris proper. Bougival's *halte* (see section 16), just upriver of the lock, is conveniently close to the town, which has an extensive market on Wednesday and Saturday mornings. The other pontoon, Halte de Plaisance de Chatou (section 16), is another 4 km upriver, on the same side. Within a short walk of this pontoon (just upriver beyond the bridge) is La Maison Fournaise, a 19th century inn which was a meeting place for many great Impressionist painters, including Monet, Manet, Degas and Renoir. Alphonse Fournaise, originally a boat carpenter, opened a boat-hire business and then took over the adjoining hotel and restaurant. Today, La Maison Fournaise is the only surviving *guinguette* where Parisians would dance, wine and dine beside the river. These days, the restored Maison Fournaise also houses a museum, documenting the place as it was 100 years ago, when Renoir set up his easel on the balcony to paint *The Luncheon of the Boating Party*.

As an alternative to passing through one of the locks at Bougival, craft can continue upriver for another 4 km and enter the Chatou lock (see section 15). This bypasses both Haltes de Plaisance, and, in terms of distance, there is nothing in it. It can take a little longer to pass through Chatou lock, as there is only one chamber here, and some of the more heavily laden barges prefer this route, because there is more water on this side of the Seine.

Bougival, Chatou and particularly Argenteuil were much painted by Claude Monet, whose pictures show elegant bathing parties, regattas, and a river bordered by beautiful countryside. Industry then sprawled out from Paris. However, these parts of the Seine are not unattractive today, with lines of poplars planted to hide the factories, and grassy banks, sometimes covered in poppies. Beyond Argenteuil, on the left bank, is Genneviliers, the largest of the three ports administered by the Port Autonome de Paris. Upstream traffic can leave the Île St Denis to port. This section is not available to downstream traffic (see plan on page 101). On the right bank is the entrance to the Canal St Denis (see section 27).

◆

24 Paris

At PK24, on the left bank, is Port Van Gogh, which is a yacht harbour, primarily used by large motor boats with their own permanent pontoon berths. Although the harbour does not really cater for visitors, it is a possible stopping place for visiting craft underway too late to make the last opening of the lock at Suresnes (PK17).

The next island, Île la Grande Jatte, provides the opportunity of escaping from the busy river traffic, and exploring another narrow backwater. Claude Monet visited the island to paint when he was living in the centre of Paris. Today, there are many smart houseboats, some with large studio windows that extend down to the level of the water. There will invariably be waves to passing boats, from diners in the waterside restaurant Martin Pêcheur.

La Défense, on the left bank and extending either side of the Pont de Neuilly (PK19), is a remarkable sight. This world-famous town-planning project is only 6 km from the Place de la Concorde, right in the centre of Paris (16 km by river). Students of architecture from all over the world come to La Défense, to climb the different levels of the central mall with its squares and patios, surrounded by vast skyscrapers, housing the head offices of many international companies. The whole scene is dominated by La Grande Arche, which could easily span Notre Dame Cathedral.

Beyond the Écluse de Suresnes (see section 15), the last of the Seine locks between Rouen and Paris, more houseboats and waterside restaurants line the river banks, within a stone's throw of the Bois de Boulogne and the famous Longchamp racecourse. Upriver of the derelict Renault works on the Île Seguin, there is the last opportunity for leaving the main thoroughfare, and slipping into the backwater behind the Île St Germain. The owners of the houseboats here are within walking distance of the centre of Paris.

The striking buildings of La Défense attract students of architecture from all over the world.

Particularly at weekends, the backwater is much used by the local rowing club, out in skiffs, fours and eights.

Arteuil, on the right bank, is a prosperous residential area, and a mixture of spacious 19th century mansion blocks with balconies and modern apartments overlooking the water. In amongst these buildings is the conspicuous Maison de Radio France, a circular white building with a high-rise tower.

The sight of the **Eiffel Tower** on the left bank, marks the entry into the heart of the capital. In the foreground, on the Allée des Cygnes, is a replica of New York's Statue of Liberty, which was donated by a group of Americans living in Paris at the end of the 19th century. Viewed for the first time from the cockpit of your own boat, the famous landmark has a special significance.

The bridges of Paris have recently undergone a facelift, as part of an ambitious plan to clean up the centre of the city. There is

The Eiffel Tower marks the start of the impressive entry into France's capital.

no mistaking the glittering bronze horses at each end of Pont Alexandre III, which was built, along with the adjoining Grand Palais with its great glass roof, to celebrate the Great Exhibition in 1900. On the right bank, just downstream of Pont Alexandre III, is a permanently-moored ship now used by the Touring Club de France. There is also a nearby fuelling pontoon (see section 17), administered by the TCF, and providing the only alongside fuelling facilities for pleasure craft in Paris, downstream of the Port de Plaisance.

The surroundings are impressive by any reckoning, with the Jardin des Tuileries and the vast Louvre Palace on one side, and the Assemblée Nationale and Musée d'Orsay (a converted railway station) on the other. With the yacht harbour only another 2 km upriver, there are more notable landmarks – on the left bank a great dome identifies the Institut de France building, with the 18th century mint (Hôtel des Monnaies) alongside. Pont Neuf, linking the Île de la Cité to the left and right banks, is the oldest of the bridges of Paris, dating back to 1578. On the Île de la Cité, there are magnificent Gothic palaces, with great towers above the

Upstream view of Pont Alexandre III, with the Eiffel Tower in the distance.

Palais de Justice, La Conciergerie and Ste Chapelle. At the other end of the Île de la Cité is perhaps the second most famous of the Parisian landmarks – Notre Dame Cathedral.

For all river traffic, there is a one-way system through the Bras de la Cité and Bras St Louis. Traffic lights on Pont au Change allow passage upstream, on the hour to 20 minutes past the hour. Downstream traffic is controlled by lights on Pont Sully, allowing access to the Bras St Louis, between 35 minutes and 50 minutes past the hour (see map on page 103). There are no restrictions for upstream traffic, if taking the narrow spur (Bras de la Monnaie), and leaving Île de la Cité to port. Those who opt for this alternative must be warned that they will not be popular with the *Bateaux Mouches*, who charge down the one-way Bras de la Monnaie, oblivious to anything else on the water. This section is closed if the river is running particularly fast. The Bras Marie is closed at all times to all craft, except for the *Bateaux Mouches*.

25 Port de Plaisance de Paris–Arsenal

Port de Plaisance

Lock dimensions
Length: 38.5 m; width: 7.6 m

Maximum boat dimensions
Length: 25 m; Draught: 1.9 m; Headroom: 4.27 m

Approach and entry

Once past Notre Dame Cathedral, the waiting pontoon is clearly visible on the right bank, outside the Port de Plaisance de Paris-Arsenal. On the pontoon is push-button communication with the Capitainerie, who have a picture on closed-circuit TV of any craft moored alongside the pontoon, awaiting entry. The Capitainerie staff will advise the new arrival to stand by for the green light, indicating that the lock is open for entry. The lights clearly show whether the opening is for commercial or pleasure craft. Once through the lock, you should moor alongside the Capitainerie pontoon, and then visit the office in order to be allocated a berth.

The Capitainerie is open:

May, June, September 0900–1900 (2000 at weekends)
July, August 0800–2000.

Access after hours
The lock can be opened by remote control after the above hours until 2300, by the lock-keeper in the office by the first of the locks (Écluses du Temple) on the Canal St Martin. The push-button intercom and closed-circuit TV picture of the pontoon are relayed to the Temple locks, after the Capitainerie has closed. It must, however, be emphasised that 'after hours' access to the Port de Plaisance will only be possible if adequate notice has been given of an intended late arrival. For reasons of security, the lock-keeper on the Canal St Martin is not permitted to open up the Port de Plaisance lock, giving access from the Seine, without prior arrangement. Any boatowner intending to arrive outside the Port de Plaisance before 2300, but after the Capitainerie has closed, should contact the Capitainerie in advance by phone (01 43 41 39 32), advising the office of the name of the boat, owner and expected time of arrival. This information is then passed on to the Écluses du Temple.

Moor up in the centre of Paris in the Port de Plaisance de Paris-Arsenal. It is sited just off the Place de la Bastille, and only 20 minutes' walk from Notre Dame.

The attractions and facilities at Port de Plaisance

Those who have not visited the Port de Plaisance de Paris-Arsenal before, may be pleasantly surprised by their surroundings. At the bottom end of the Canal St Martin, what was originally a commercial basin was redeveloped for pleasure use in 1983, and now features in many guide books to Paris as a tourist attraction. The tree-lined ramparts, on the west side of the basin, were part of the fortifications that surrounded Paris in the 14th century. On the other side are attractively landscaped gardens, including a *roserie*. At the top end of the Port de Plaisance is the Bastille Métro station, over the tunnel that runs beneath the Place de la Bastille and provides access to the Canal St Martin.

Showers, washing machines and a telephone are located in the Capitainerie building (open 0600–2300), with additional facilities on the other side of the basin. Small shops, including several *boulangeries*, and a couple of garages, are to be found in the back-streets behind the Capitainerie, or on the other side, in the direction of the Seine. The nearest supermarket is in the rue St Antoine and there is a yacht chandler at the beginning of rue des Filles du Calvaire which is a continuation of Bd Beaumarchais and about 15 minutes' walk from the yacht harbour.

Security around the yacht basin is strict, with no public access between 2300 and 0800.

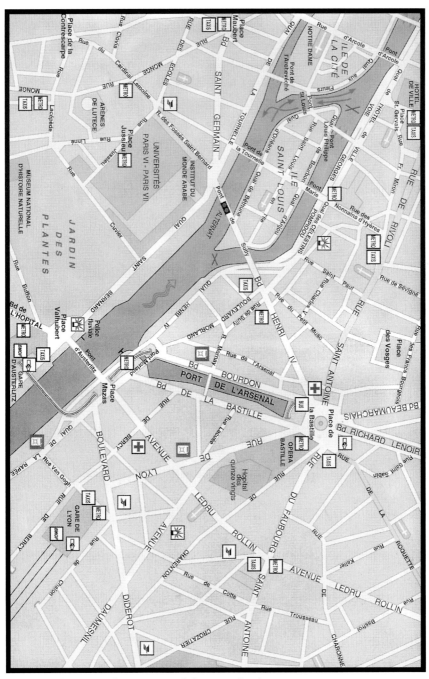

A plan of the area of Paris around the Port de Plaisance.
© APEX Cartographie.

Anyone moored in the Port de Plaisance de Paris-Arsenal is right in the centre of Paris, within 20 minutes' walk from Notre Dame. For those who want to stroll the Champs-Elysées, visit the Louvre Museum, or climb up to the Basilique de Sacré Coeur to explore Montmartre, there are two Metro stations (Bastille, line 1 and Quai de la Rapée, line 5), conveniently close by.

There is plenty to do and see around the yacht basin. The Place de la Bastille is dominated by the Colonne de Juillet, a 52 m column with the gleaming bronze figure of Liberty, symbolically breaking her chains, on the top (clearly visible from the Port de Plaisance). The column was built as a memorial to those who died in the peasant uprisings in July 1830 when, in three days of street fighting, the King was deposed and replaced by Louis-Philippe. The Bastille area has become popular with tourists, who pack the many restaurants and bars around the square until the early morning. Here too is the Opéra de la Bastille, which opened on Bastille Day 1989 as part of the bicentenary celebrations of the French Revolution.

Off the Place de la Bastille, the Boulevard Richard Lenoir has many excellent shops, and there is a busy market in the middle of the Boulevard, beneath the trees which once lined the sides of the first part of the Canal St Martin, now contained within the 2 km tunnel below. The rue de la Roquette and the rue de Lappe, on the east side of the square, are packed with bars and restaurants, some with distinctive Spanish décor and menus. This area is much patronised at night by Parisians.

Depending on how much time you have in Paris, there is much to be said for using the boat for a day's sightseeing tour of the capital. From the Port de Plaisance there are several options, which are described in Part III: The Canals of Paris.

PART III
The Canals of Paris

·····················◆·····················

26 History of the Paris Canals

Much of today's 120 km network of canals was conceived by Napoleon, and has been administered by the City of Paris since 1802, when work started on the Canal de l'Ourcq.

The Ourcq river was canalised back in 1520 by François I, so that supplies of wood and stone could be transported to Paris from the heart of the countryside. The boats used were 32 m *flutes* or *demi-flutes*, so named because they were exceptionally narrow. The one-way journey was extremely hazardous, for there were no conventional locks, only a series of 21 *pertuis* or weirs. These were blocked with timber, which had to be withdrawn to provide a gap for the loaded boats to shoot over the top of the weir and plunge down to the lower level. Later on, adjoining weirs were built to reduce the fall, but there were still, in the 16th and 17th centuries, many broken boats, injuries and drownings. At the end of the 'canalised' Ourcq, the river traffic joined the fast-flowing Marne river, which carried the survivors into the capital, where the boats would be destroyed, as there was no means of making the return trip. Conventional locks were introduced in the 18th century, but the *flutes* and *demi-flutes* were never fitted with engines, and as late as 1960 they relied on the current for the downriver passage, using horses, and then tractors, for the return trip.

A new waterway – the Canal de l'Ourcq, linking the canalised Ourcq with Paris – was started by Napoleon in 1802, taking 21 years to complete. Napoleon's plans also included the Bassin de la Villette, the Canal St Martin and the Canal St Denis, linking the Ourcq with the Seine. The prime purpose of Napoleon's Ourcq canal system was to provide Paris with drinking water, and a less hazardous means of moving wood, stone, sugar beet and flour into the capital.

The Port de Plaisance end of the Canal St Martin was enclosed in 1835 for military purposes, to provide the army with free movement in or out of the city, where, five years earlier, uprisings, barricades and revolution were rife. The 'vault' or tunnel was extended in 1906 to 2 km.

There are sections of the Canal de l'Ourcq that are within a stone's throw of the Marne river, where the original drainage and pumping stations maintain the water level. The canal was abandoned as a source of supply of drinking water in 1832, after an outbreak of cholera, but to this day the Ourcq provides the water for the public gardens and for cleaning the streets of Paris. At the Paris end of the Canal de l'Ourcq, the vast Bassin de la Villette acts as a reservoir, which also maintains the water levels in the St Martin and St Denis canals. In order to satisfy this constant demand for water, two remarkable feats of engineering still lift water 12 m from the Marne river and pump it into the Canal de l'Ourcq. Both *usines élévatoire* are open to the public.

A plan is under consideration to link the Marne to the Canal de l'Ourcq, by providing a boat-lift close to the Villers-les-Rigault pumping station.

The locks along the Canal de l'Ourcq were originally designed with two chambers to accommodate the increasing commercial traffic. This allowed the locks to be prepared in advance for a 23m mail boat, which plied between Meaux and Paris between 1837 and 1860. The hull was built in Scotland and fitted out in France for carrying passengers in comfort. Pulled by horses, with uniformed riders carrying a flaming torch and sounding a hunting horn to announce the boat's imminent arrival, the *Bateaux-Poste*, with priority over all other craft, completed the 48 km passage in 3½ hours.

With the decline in commercial traffic, the Canal de l'Ourcq was closed in 1960, and there was a plan drawn up to fill in the waterway, to provide a motorway into the heart of Paris. This plan was dropped when one of the passenger-boat operators, using the Canal St Martin, was able to demonstrate that water-tourism could work on the waterways where pleasure craft had previously been excluded.

The Mayor of Paris decided that the city should invest huge amounts of money to re-open the entire length of the Canal de l'Ourcq and the canalised Ourcq for pleasure use. After 20 years of neglect, the Ourcq waterways were re-opened in 1983, along with the Port de Plaisance de Paris-Arsenal – the capital's first yacht harbour.

The locks are gradually being made fully automatic along the Canal de l'Ourcq, as more and more pleasure boats and passenger-boats take to these waters.

······················◆······················

27 Cruising possibilities: Canal St Martin • Bassin de la Villette • Canal St Denis

Anyone planning to spend a few days in the Port de Plaisance should consider taking the boat for evening or day trips on the Paris canals. For those who have tired of trudging round the tourist sites on foot, faces buried in guide books, this can provide a delightful opportunity for sampling something different.

You can cruise between the Port de Plaisance and the Bassin de la Villette, or take a day's sightseeing tour from the Port de Plaisance, taking in the tunnel and Canal St Martin, Bassin de la Villette and Canal St Denis, and returning up the Seine in the evening to the same berth in the Port de Plaisance. Alternatively, the sightseeing circuit can be made in the opposite direction.

THE CANALS OF PARIS

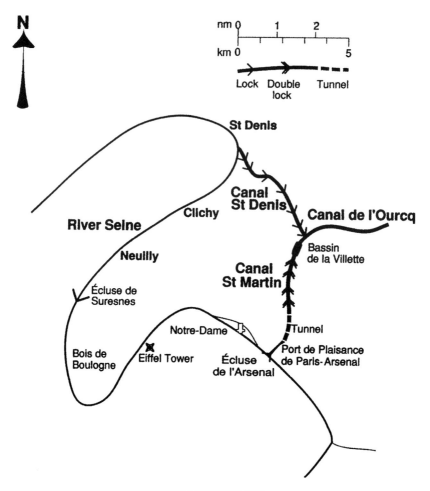

				Boat restrictions		
	Length	*Length*	*Height*	*Draught*	*No of*	*Operating*
	km	m	m	m	*locks*	*times*
Canal St Martin	4.5	25	4.27	1.9	1 single 4 double	0800–2345*
Canal St Denis	6.6	30	4.44	2.6	7	0630–2130
River Seine between St Denis and Port de Plaisance de Paris-Arsenal	28.9	180	6.0	3.0	1	0700–1900

*Port de Plaisance de Paris-Arsenal: lock only opened after 1900/2000 by prior arrangement (see section 25)

Note: this sight-seeing tour of Paris is possible only if the boat's draught does not exceed 1.9 m and the height is less than 4.27 m. (See page 66.)

Canal St Martin

Although the Canal St Martin is only 4.5 km in length, boatowners should reckon on 2½ hours for the passage to the Bassin de la Villette. This involves passing through the 2 km vault or tunnel, and then negotiating four double locks to climb 28 m (2 m more than the climb between the sea and Paris via the Seine).

If planning to take the boat through the tunnel and along the Canal St Martin, it is essential to visit the Capitainerie who will co-ordinate the passage through the tunnel and locks with the Écluses du Temple (the first of the Canal St Martin's locks). Without this, no attempt should be made to wait off the entrance to the tunnel for a green light, which might well apply only to a *vedette*. Generally speak-

A *vedette* leaves for the Canals of Paris, entering the tunnel at the top end of the Port de Plaisance.

ing, the most likely arrangement will be for the boatowner to be at the tunnel entrance early in the day, before the start of the *vedette* traffic, which has priority. The next opportunity for passing through the tunnel may not be until later on in the afternoon. After one or two accidents in the tunnel, the traffic is strictly one-way only. You should discuss with the Capitainerie the time-table for the return passage.

The Temple lock-keeper, on his remote TV monitor, will see the yacht waiting to enter the tunnel at the agreed time, and turn on the green light. Passage through the tunnel, for many boatowners, will be a new experience. By day, the only illumination is from shafts of sunlight through ventilation holes in the roof, beneath the Boulevards Richard Lenoir and Jules Ferry. After dark, some form of light from the boat is necessary, to illuminate the roof, and pick out the long bend in the tunnel.

Towards the end of the tunnel, there may appear alarming flashing red lights, which will turn out to be friendly messages (in English if an

One of the few barges that still use the Canal St Martin, emerges from the tunnel beneath the Place de la Bastille.

English boat is expected through), saying 'Welcome to the Canals of Paris' or 'Have a Good Journey'.

Emerging, blinking in the sunlight, the Écluses du Temple will almost certainly be open for immediate entry. If returning in the evening, it can be prudent to talk to the lock-keeper on the way up, and indicate the time you expect to start the return passage from the Bassin de la Villette (which should be no later than 2100).

Although progress through the four double locks is slow, the surroundings are delightful. The canal passes through a residential area of Paris which, in recent years, has undergone a considerable face-lift, and apartments here are much sought after. There are attractive iron footbridges spanning the chestnut-lined canal. The area is much used for locations for film and TV. Several *Maigret* episodes were filmed here, along with *Last Tango in Paris*. On the right-hand-side going up the canal, just beyond the second double lock (Écluses des Recollets) is the façade of the Hôtel du Nord, which was the inspiration for the film of the same name, and a famous scene during which the main characters exchange much-quoted dialogue, standing on one of the footbridges above the canal (actually recreated in the studio). The front of the Hôtel du Nord (saved from demolition by film historians) can still be seen from the canal.

Bassin de la Villette

Emerging from the last lock, a boat enters the vast Bassin de la Villette. To the left are the canal offices and a fleet of self-drive hire boats; to the right are the passenger-boats that make regular trips between the Bassin de la Villette and the Port de Plaisance de Paris-Arsenal. This is also an embarkation point for the cruises along the Canal de l'Ourcq between Villette and Meaux (see section 30).

Continuing up the basin, under the footbridge, the remarkable raising Pont de Crimée will be seen ahead. It is necessary to keep over to the right-hand-side of the basin, where, on the corner of a large warehouse, is a light beam which, when broken by passage of a boat, brings down the traffic barriers and starts the lift wheels of this remarkable ancient bridge which dates back to 1885. Approaching the bridge from the other direction, the light beam is just above the water, in the wall of the quay. At both points, there are notices, in English, indicating how to use your boat to raise the bridge.

At the end of the Bassin de la Villette, off to the left, is the Canal St Denis. Ahead is the start of the Canal de l'Ourcq where, on the right, there is plenty of space to moor up alongside, avoiding the areas reserved for the passenger-boats. On this side of the canal there is parkland. On the other side is the shining silver globe of La Géode (a vast cinema, using the latest projection techniques to show scientific films), and behind this is the Cité des Sciences et de l'Industrie.

A light beam operates the lifting Pont de Crimée which spans the Bassin de la Villette.

Part of the Cité des Sciences et de l'Industrie, which can be reached by boats in the Port de Plaisance de Paris-Arsenal via the tunnel.

The land now occupied by the Cité des Sciences et de l'Industrie complex was originally a cattle market and abattoir. The whole area on both sides of the canal was the scene of development on a grand scale, during the 1980s. Located in the landscaped parkland and gardens is Le Zénith, accommodating audiences of several thousand and used primarily for rock concerts. The Grande Halle, originally built for cattle auctions, now houses exhibitions and displays. There is a concert hall, theatre, music school, two pavilions for children and several restaurants.

The Cité, on the other side of the canal, occupying 10 acres, is a modern structure of blue girders and glass, all surrounded by a moat. The building is in four sections, with each section having several different levels. The main attraction, *Explora*, consists of four permanent exhibitions: *The Adventure of Life, From the Earth to the Universe, Matter and the Work of Man* and *Language and Communication*. Anyone could easily spend a day in one section and still not cover everything. For those with only an hour or two to spare, the Museum authorities suggest viewing an orbital space station, the Ariane rocket and a Nautilus submarine, all located in *From the Earth to the Universe*. If there is still time, a visit to the Planetarium is recommended. For children in various age groups there are special scientific displays in which they can participate.

For those skippers with crews not inclined to immerse themselves in scientific exhibitions, a late afternoon departure from the Port de Plaisance, with an evening meal in one of the many restaurants around the Bassin de la Villette, may have more appeal. Motoring back along the canal, in the gathering darkness, and then through the tunnel, does have a certain fascination. Departure should be before 2100, otherwise entry into the first of the canal locks may not be permitted.

A more ambitious sightseeing tour, again from foredeck, cockpit or bridge of one's own yacht or motorboat, is to spend a whole day and evening doing a complete circuit of Paris, starting from and finishing at the Port de Plaisance de Paris-Arsenal. If the circuit is taken anti-clockwise, this involves passage-making along the full lengths of the Canal St Martin and Canal St Denis and then returning to base along the River Seine.

Before setting out on the circuit described above, it is vital to consult with the Capitainerie and make an early entry into the tunnel, before the *vedettes* monopolise the Canal St Martin. As the boat will almost certainly be locking back into the Port de Plaisance after the Capitainerie has closed, make sure that they advise the Temple lock-keeper of the estimated time of arrival (which must be before 2300), on the pontoon in the Seine adjacent to the Port de Plaisance lock. Without this advance information, the lock will not be remotely opened up, to regain access into the Port de Plaisance. As a precaution, hand the Temple lock-keeper a note stating the name of your boat and the estimated time of arrival.

Canal St Denis

The advantage of completing this sightseeing circuit in an anti-clockwise direction is that you can stop off for a leisurely lunch in the Bassin de la Villette, before navigating the Canal St Denis (6.6 km – 7 locks). The first of the Canal St Denis locks, just off the Bassin de la Villette, was constructed by Napoleon, and is remarkable in that boats enter over the top of the gate, which then slowly emerges from the water astern.

The temptation will be to press on along the Canal St Denis which is mainly industrial, and, with each of the locks having two chambers, there will usually be little delay. All the St Denis canal locks have been modernised, to take an increasing amount of barge traffic carrying building materials. The locks have two control centres, one at each end of the canal. Each lock, remotely controlled, has eight closed-circuit TV cameras, along with press-button intercom for those boats without VHF (Ch 20). A small charge is levied at the last lock. Much of the town of St Denis is industrial, but it also has one of the finest examples of a Gothic basilica in France, where most of the nation's monarchs are buried.

It will take about 1½ hours to cover the Canal St Denis, and the passage must be planned to lock out into the Seine in good time to complete the next 12 km (7.5 nm) along the Seine, between St Denis and the lock at Suresnes (see section 15), which closes at 1900.

Once through Suresnes, a vessel has to pass through the industrial suburbs of Paris before reaching the Eiffel Tower, the magnificent bridges and, of course, the famous city sights like Notre Dame Cathedral. If one's boat dawdles, Paris can be entered at dusk, when many of the waterside buildings are illuminated. The *Bateaux Mouches*, covered in fairy lights, glide by, some with passengers dining in style by candlelight. These boats really do have searchlights, which are used to pick out couples beside the river. Arriving on the illuminated pontoon, outside the Port de Plaisance at the appointed hour, the Temple lock-keeper is contacted on the push-button intercom (also available on Ch 20). Entry should soon be gained to return to the berth, left, perhaps, 14–16 hours earlier.

Although completing the circuit in a clockwise direction misses out on seeing Paris after dark, there are some advantages. An early departure from the Port de Plaisance is not so essential, and the river sights in central Paris can be viewed at leisure during the morning. Again, it is recommended that the plan is discussed with the Capitainerie, who should advise the Temple lock-keeper that the boat will be wanting to enter the Canal St Martin from the Bassin de la Villette in the late after-noon or evening (at the latest 2100). Depending on the time a boat leaves the Port de Plaisance, and progress down the Seine and along the Canal St Denis, much of the afternoon and evening could be spent in the Bassin de la Villette, perhaps including a visit to the Cité des Sciences et de l'Industrie and an evening meal, before returning to the Port de Plaisance along the Canal St Martin.

············◆············

28 Cruising possibilities: Canal de l'Ourcq • Canalised Ourcq river

The opportunity of seeing the Ourcq in one's own boat will almost certainly be restricted to the **Grande Section** (11 km), where there is 2.6 m of water. In the Petite Section (97 km), the minimum depth is 0.8 m. The Canal Authority state that there may be 1.1 m depth (at the owner's risk), but regular users claim that over some short sections there can even be slightly less than 0.8 m.

The Grande Section of the Canal de l'Ourcq cannot really be recom-mended for boats which, because of their draught, can make no further progress upstream, beyond the first lock at Sevran and into the Petite Section. The 11 km of the Grande Section is a mixture of factories (some derelict), new offices, and parkland. The lines of poplars achieve some screening, but the general impression is of being in the industrial outskirts of Paris. Working barges still use this section of the canal.

Users of the spectacularly beautiful **Petite Section** of the Canal de l'Ourcq will almost certainly be restricted to self-drive hire boats, small

CANAL DE L'OURCQ

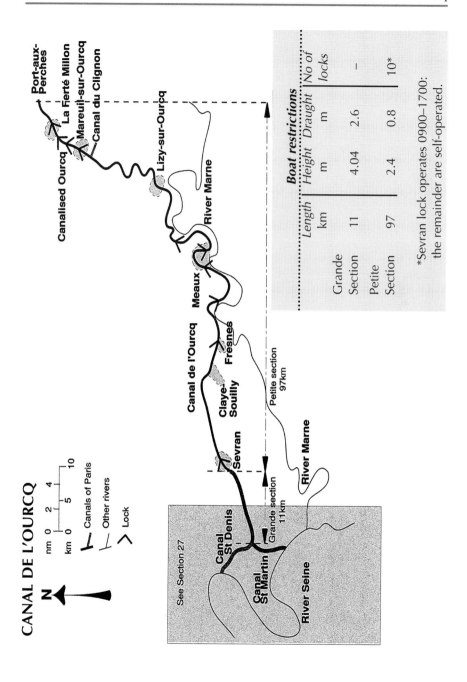

	Length km	Height m	Draught m	No of locks
Grande Section	11	4.04	2.6	–
Petite Section	97	2.4	0.8	10*

Boat restrictions

*Sevran lock operates 0900–1700: the remainder are self-operated.

The tranquil waters of the Petite Section of the Canal de l'Ourcq.

motorboats towed to one of the launching ramps listed on page 79, and the sightseeing passenger-boats (see section 30).

Those able to navigate the Petite Section of the Ourcq in their own boat must have a *permis*, available from one of the waterway offices located at:

5 quai de la Loire	6 avenue de General Gallieni,
Bassin de la Villette	77100 Meaux
75019 Paris	Tel: 1 60 09 95 00
Tel: 1 44 89 15 15	

The above offices hand over a key to operate the locks and lifting bridges, and to gain access to shower blocks along the way. They will also provide a detailed booklet explaining in detail how to operate the various locks and lifting bridges. Use of the waterways is free for the first seven days.

Upstream of the Sevran lock, a boat is already in the Petite Section of the Ourcq, where the waterway narrows into a long straight section, lined with poplars on both sides and spanned by many small bridges. The towpath is mostly for the benefit of energetic cyclists.

Claye-Souilly (PK27) is the first possible stopping place, by which time the crew will have already savoured the delightful surroundings, as the canal bends first in one direction and then the other, through the wooded countryside. There are mooring posts either side of Claye-Souilly's lifting bridge. This is the main base for Sinope Evasion's fleet of self-drive motor cruisers. There are showers here and fuel pumps for alongside fuelling (the only place on the Ourcq where this is possible). The bars and restaurants, overlooking the canal, cater for passengers aboard the *Canauxrama vedette* that stops here over lunch-time. There are shops and the usual facilities in the town's main street.

At **Fresnes-sur-Marne** (PK32), there are mooring posts on the bank by a designated picnic area, provided by the waterway authority. This is a village with a restaurant near the canal.

Beyond the second lock – Écluse de Fresnes (PK33) – the canal and the river Marne are within a short distance of each other. Having pushed aside the Pont du Parc's creepers, which cover the whole bridge and almost reach the water, there are mooring posts to use, so that one may visit the Usine Élévatoire de Trilbardou, the remarkable pumping station built in 1869, and still lifting water 12 m from the Marne to the Canal de l'Ourcq.

Anyone who is looking for more signs of civilisation will want to stop off in the old city of **Meaux** (PK48), which is served by both the Canal de l'Ourcq and the Marne river. Situated between two locks, Écluse de Villenoy and Écluse St Lazare, not a great deal of the city is to be seen from the canal, but there are plenty of places to moor up, and then explore the place on foot. Showers are available at Ourcq Cruiser Hire, above Écluse de Villenoy, and the waterway office (location marked on the canal bank with a prominent 'i' sign) is close by.

After the Varreddes lock (PK65) is the Usine Élévatoire de Villers-les-Rigault, another pumping station, where a barrage turns the water-wheel, to pump water from the Marne to the Canal de l'Ourcq, 12 m above. It is similar to the one at Trilbardou and was built around the same time. Mooring posts here allow one to visit it.

Another 1.5 km upstream of the pumping station, the Marne, river Ourcq and Canal de l'Ourcq are almost alongside each other, except for the difference in levels. There are mooring posts here, next to the original steps leading down from the canal to the rivers below. This is the point where cargoes were manually trans-shipped between the canal and river, under the supervision of officials based at the nearby cream-painted Maison du Confluent. Plans are currently under consideration to install a boat-lift here, so that boats can be moved from one waterway to another. In terms of water tourism, this could represent a week-long cruise, without ever having to cover the same stretch of waterway. A possible itinerary might start at the Port de Plaisance de Paris-Arsenal in the centre of Paris, joining the Marne to the south of Paris, a transfer of the boat by lift onto the Canal de l'Ourcq, thence to the Bassin de la Villette and the Canal St Martin to complete the circuit.

There is little to see at **Lizy-sur-Ourcq** (PK77), apart from some modest industrial development. It can, however, be a useful place to stop for shopping, with a nearby *supermarché* and the usual facilities of a small town. It was at Lizy-sur-Ourcq that the distinctive waterway *flutes* and *demi-flutes* were built. Still to be seen on the waterway, they are mostly

A traditional *demi-flute* workboat at Mareuil-sur-Ourcq.

used to carry out maintenance work on the canal banks.

The Canal du Clignon (PK93), off to the right and just downstream of **Mareuil-sur-Ourcq** (PK96), is navigable for just 1.2 km, until blocked by a low bridge. There is a turning circle here which is a mere 12 m across. At one point, an aqueduct carries the canal over the Ourcq river. At the end of the canal, beyond the low bridge, is the privately-owned La Commanderie. There is 0.8 m water in the Canal du Clignon, and providing the skipper is confident of being able to manoeuvre within the restricted turning circle, this can provide an interesting deviation from the Canal de l'Ourcq.

Before the lock at Mareuil-sur-Ourcq the canal opens up with quays on both sides. To the left is the embarkation point for the passenger-boats operated by Un Canal ... Deux Canaux, and there is plenty of room alongside for visiting boats. On the other side is the base for six self-drive motor cruisers, operated by Rivière et Canaux de France, who established themselves here in 1997. Just beyond the base is a weir, and the end of the navigable Ourcq river. Once through Mareuil's lock, a boat has left the Canal de l'Ourcq and enters the last 10 km of waterway – the canalised Ourcq river.

La Ferté-Milon (PK104) is dominated by the towering remains of the 14th century Château de Louis d'Orléans and circled by five towers which were part of the defences of the ancient town. The tiny Île de Mail, between the original Ourcq river and the canal, has been administered by the City of Paris since the 19th century, when a young Parisian engineer called Eiffel designed the metal footbridge to the island, where the townsfolk now gather to enjoy the tranquil surroundings. There are the remains of a water-mill here, originally used for grinding flour. Arguments often broke out between the mill owner and those who worked on the water, whose boats, caught in the strong current, frequently breached the weir barrier, leaving the mill with no source of power until the damage had been repaired.

Part of the old fortifications of the delightful old town of La Ferté-Milon.

Navigation is not possible beyond Port-aux-Perches, where the Ourcq river belongs to the fishermen and wildfowl. Port-aux-Perches is on the outskirts of the small village of Silly-la-Pôterie. There is nothing here except for a large house at the end of the waterway, which is rented by the City of Paris to the passenger-boat operators *Un Canal ... Deux Canaux*, who start many of their river cruises from here. They have also built a grand restaurant which is gaining a reputation and attracting visitors from Paris (one hour by car).

29 Boat hire

Several companies now operate fleets of self-drive motorboats from bases on the Petite Section of the Canal de l'Ourcq and the Bassin de la Villette. No *permis* is required to drive a hired boat. Details are available from:

Sinope Evasion	Nicols
Port de Plaisance	Route du Puy St Bonnet
77410 Claye-Souilly	49300 Cholet
Tel: 1 60 27 05 51	Tel: 2 41 56 46 56
	(bases at Meaux, on both the Canal de l'Ourcq and the Marne river)

Ourcq Loisirs
9 quai de la Loire
Bassin de la Villette
75019 Paris
Tel: 42 40 82 10
(bases at Bassin de la Villette
and Meaux)

Rivière et Canaux de France
Port de Plaisance de Chauny
Rue du Port
02300 Chauny
Tel: 2 23 39 21 21
(base at Mareuil-sur-Ourcq)

◆

30 Pleasure boat trips and cruises

Paris

Crews of boats in the Port de Plaisance de Paris-Arsenal might like to consider taking one of the 2½ hour *Canauxrama* boat trips from the yacht harbour, through the tunnel under the Place de Bastille, and along the Canal St Martin, seeing parts of Paris not normally on the tourist-beaten track. The boat trips finish (or start in the opposite direction) at the Bassin de la Villette, within walking distance of the Cité des Sciences et de l'Industrie (see section 27).

Canal de l'Ourcq

Those who want to make a day trip along the Canal de l'Ourcq and see something of the French countryside should consider another *Canauxrama* cruise, which involves a transfer from coach to boat, or boat to coach, just downstream of the Vignely lock outside Meaux. These cruises start or finish at the Bassin de la Villette, and include a long stop for lunch and a visit to the pumping station at Trilbardou.

Canauxrama
Bassin de la Villette
13 quai de la Loire
75019 Paris
Tel: 1 42 39 15 00

To explore the upper reaches of the Canal de l'Ourcq and canalised l'Ourcq, Un Canal ... Deux Canaux have cruises of various lengths, some with meals included, starting from Port-aux-Perches, La Ferté-Milon, Varreddes or Lizy-sur-Ourq on Saturdays, Sundays and national holidays.

Port-aux-Perches can be your starting place for a pleasure cruise on the
navigable canalised Ourcq river.

Un Canal ... Deux Canaux
Port-aux-Perches
02460 Silly la Pôterie
Tel: 3 23 96 41 25

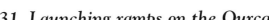

31 *Launching ramps on the Ourcq*

Owners of small motorboats, towed overland with a view to launching in
the Petite Section of the Ourcq, will find convenient launching ramps at:

* Pavillons-sous-Bois
* Claye-Souilly
* Meaux – Saint-Rémy
* Varreddes
* Mareuil-sur-Ourcq
* La Ferté-Milon

The boat must not be launched without having obtained a *permis* from
one of the waterway offices shown on page 74. Canoes, rowing boats or
sailing dinghies are not permitted to use these waterways.

PART IV
Sectional maps
of the Seine

from the estuary to Paris

SEINE ESTUARY

Important note:

Pleasure craft must not enter the buoyed shipping channel in the Chenal de Rouen. Instead pass port to port, keeping just outside the port hand buoys for the entire section between buoy No 4 and Tancarville bridge; this is a distance of 16.5 nm.

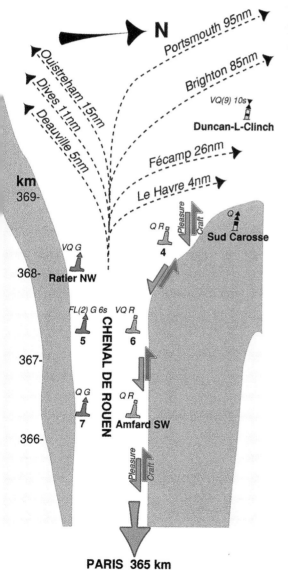

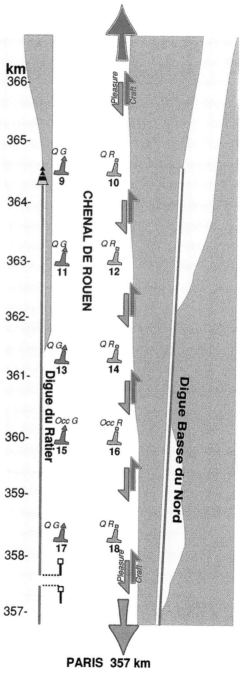

81

KEY TO SYMBOLS

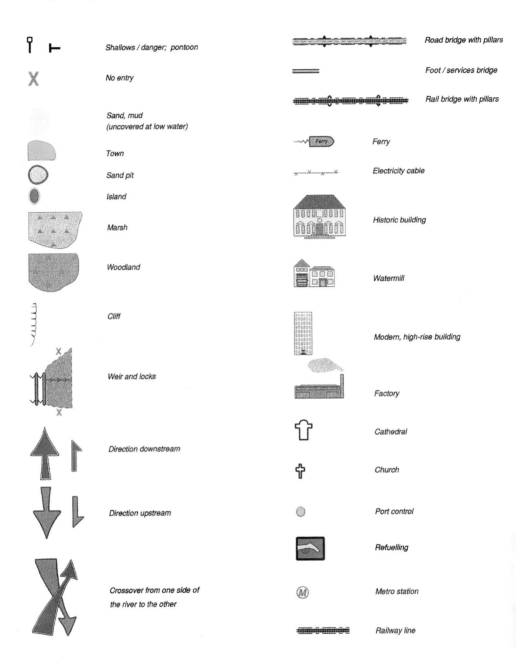

Shallows / danger; pontoon

No entry

Sand, mud
(uncovered at low water)

Town

Sand pit

Island

Marsh

Woodland

Cliff

Weir and locks

Direction downstream

Direction upstream

Crossover from one side of
the river to the other

Road bridge with pillars

Foot / services bridge

Rail bridge with pillars

Ferry

Electricity cable

Historic building

Watermill

Modern, high-rise building

Factory

Cathedral

Church

Port control

Refuelling

Metro station

Railway line

Note: The figures in brackets next to place names on the maps refer to the text section numbers.

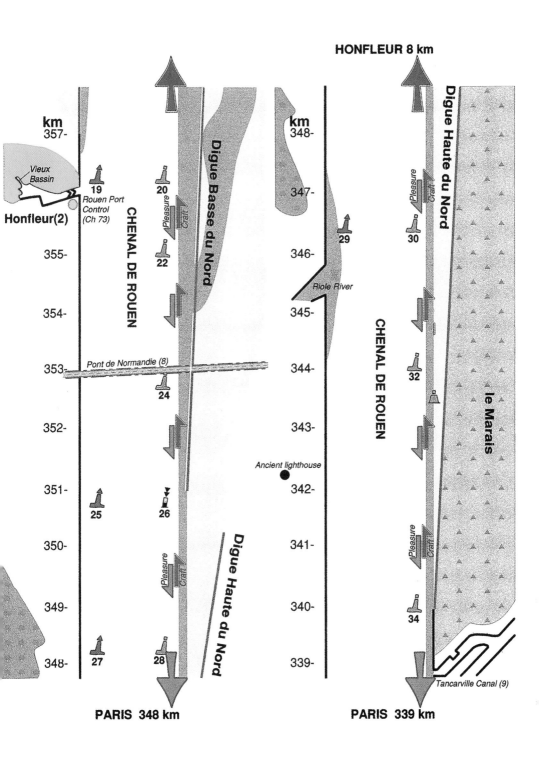

HONFLEUR 8 km

Digue Haute du Nord

km
357-

*Vieux
Bassin*

19
*Rouen Port
Control
(Ch 73)*

Honfleur(2)

CHENAL DE ROUEN

20

Pleasure

Craft

Digue Basse du Nord

km
348-

347-

Pleasure

Craft

30

355-

22

Pleasure

29

Riole River

346-

354-

345-

353- *Pont de Normandie (8)*

344-

CHENAL DE ROUEN

32

24

352-

343-

Ancient lighthouse

351-

25

26

342-

Digue Haute du Nord

Pleasure

Craft

350-

341-

Pleasure

Craft

349-

340-

34

348- 27

28

339-

Tancarville Canal (9)

le Marais

PARIS 348 km

PARIS 339 km

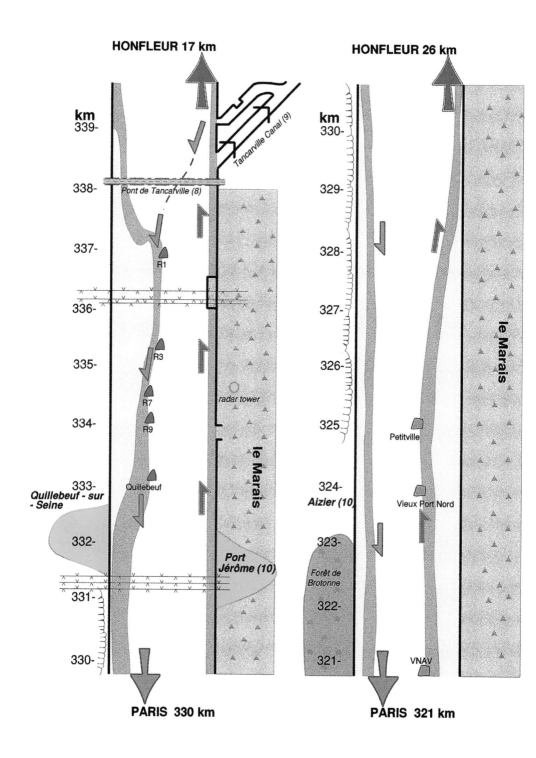

HONFLEUR 17 km

HONFLEUR 26 km

km
339-

km
330-

Tancarville Canal (9)

338-

Pont de Tancarville (8)

329-

337-

R1

328-

336-

327-

335-

R3

326-

R7

radar tower

334-

R9

325-

Petitville

le Marais

333-

Quillebeuf

le Marais

324-

Quillebeuf - sur - Seine

Aizier (10)

Vieux Port Nord

332-

Port Jérôme (10)

323-

Forêt de Brotonne

331-

322-

330-

321-

VNAV

PARIS 330 km

PARIS 321 km

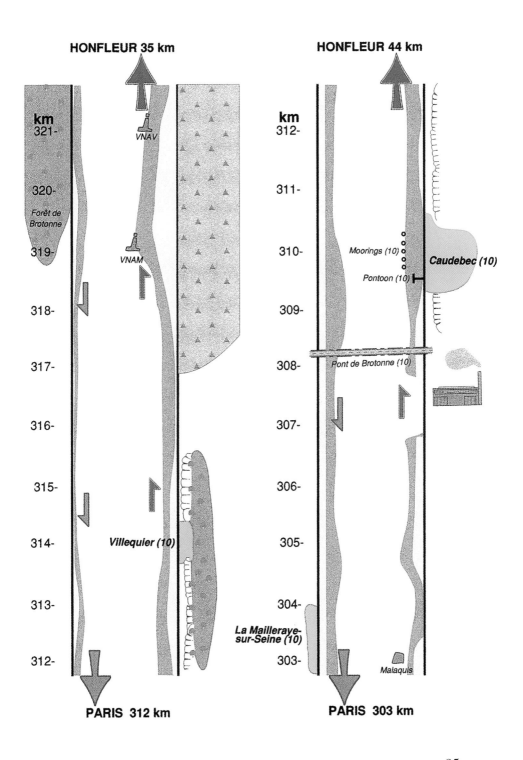

HONFLEUR 35 km

km
321-

320-

Forêt de Brotonne

319-

318-

317-

316-

315-

314-

313-

312-

VNAV

VNAM

Villequier (10)

PARIS 312 km

HONFLEUR 44 km

km
312-

311-

310-

309-

308-

307-

306-

305-

304-

303-

Moorings (10)

Caudebec (10)

Pontoon (10)

Pont de Brotonne (10)

La Mailleraye-sur-Seine (10)

Malaquis

PARIS 303 km

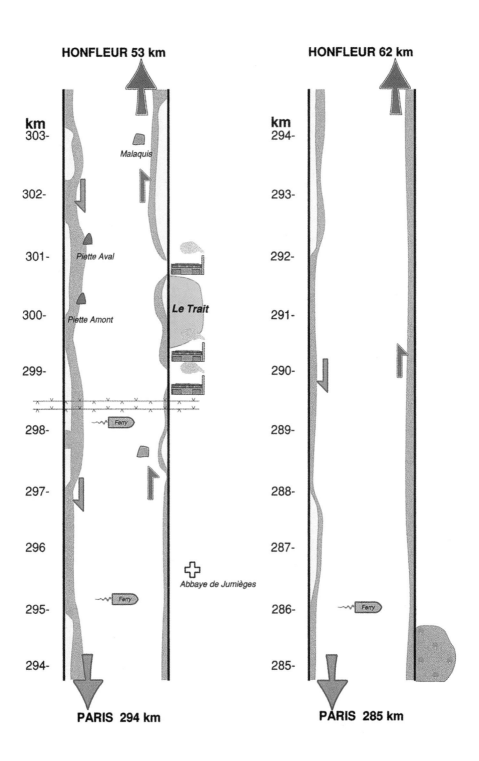

HONFLEUR 53 km

HONFLEUR 62 km

km
303-
302-
301-
300-
299-
298-
297-
296
295-
294-

km
294-
293-
292-
291-
290-
289-
288-
287-
286-
285-

Malaquis

Piette Aval

Piette Amont

Le Trait

Ferry

Ferry

Ferry

Abbaye de Jumièges

PARIS 294 km

PARIS 285 km

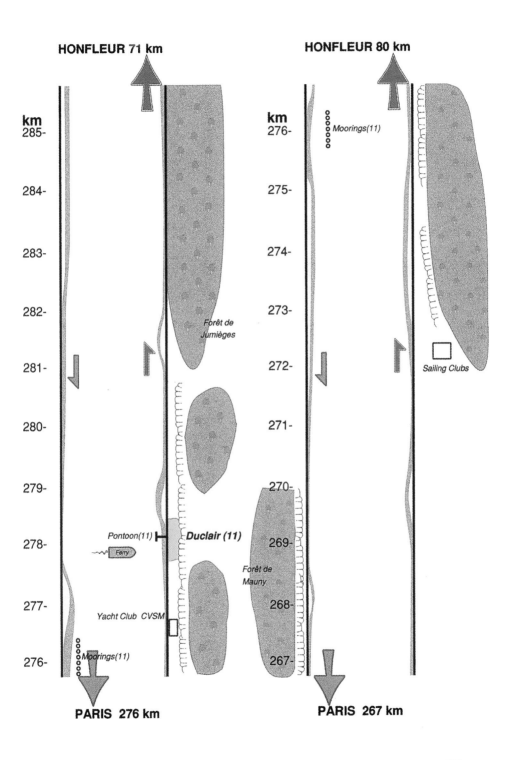

HONFLEUR 71 km

HONFLEUR 80 km

km
285-

284-

283-

282-

281-

280-

279-

278-

277-

276-

km
276-

275-

274-

273-

272-

271-

270-

269-

268-

267-

Moorings(11)

Forêt de
Jumièges

Pontoon(11) — **Duclair (11)**

Ferry

Yacht Club CVSM

Moorings(11)

Forêt de
Mauny

Sailing Clubs

PARIS 276 km

PARIS 267 km

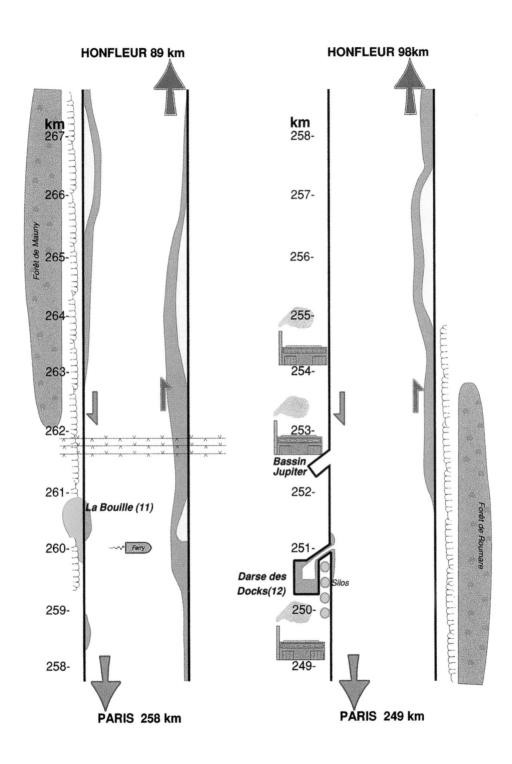

HONFLEUR 89 km

km
267-
266-
265-
264-
263-
262-
261-
260-
259-
258-

Forêt de Mauny

La Bouille (11)

Ferry

PARIS 258 km

HONFLEUR 98km

km
258-
257-
256-
255-
254-
253-
252-
251-
250-
249-

Bassin Jupiter

Darse des Docks(12)

Silos

Forêt de Roumare

PARIS 249 km

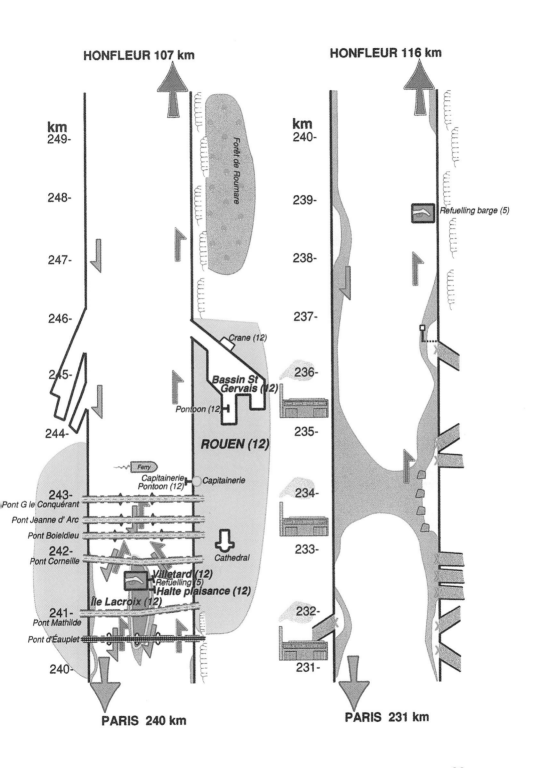

HONFLEUR 107 km

HONFLEUR 116 km

km
249-

km
240-

248-

239-

Forêt de Roumare

Refuelling barge (5)

247-

238-

246-

237-

Crane (12)

245-

236-

Bassin St Gervais (12)

Pontoon (12)

244-

235-

ROUEN (12)

Ferry

Capitainerie Pontoon (12)

Capitainerie

243-
Pont G le Conquérant

234-

Pont Jeanne d' Arc

Pont Boieldieu

242-
Pont Corneille

233-

Cathedral

Villetard (12)
Refuelling (5)
Halte plaisance (12)

Île Lacroix (12)

241-
Pont Mathilde

232-

Pont d'Éauplet

240-

231-

PARIS 240 km

PARIS 231 km

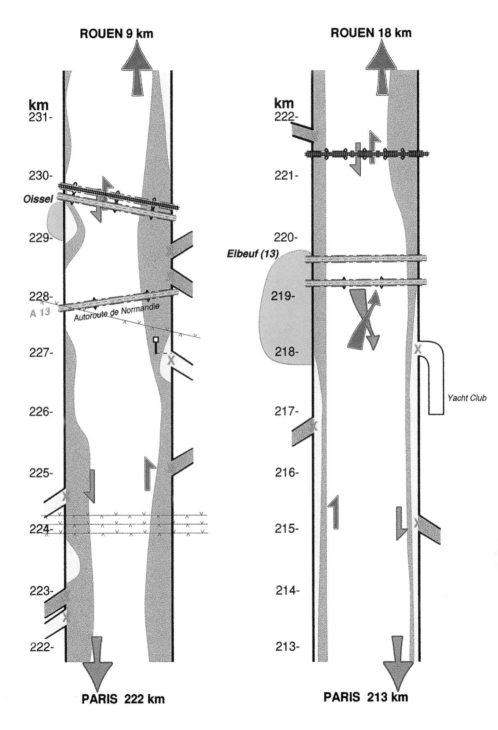

ROUEN 9 km

km
231-

230-
Oissel

229-

228-
A 13   Autoroute de Normandie

227-

226-

225-

224-

223-

222-

PARIS 222 km

ROUEN 18 km

km
222-

221-

220-
Elbeuf (13)

219-

218-

Yacht Club

217-

216-

215-

214-

213-

PARIS 213 km

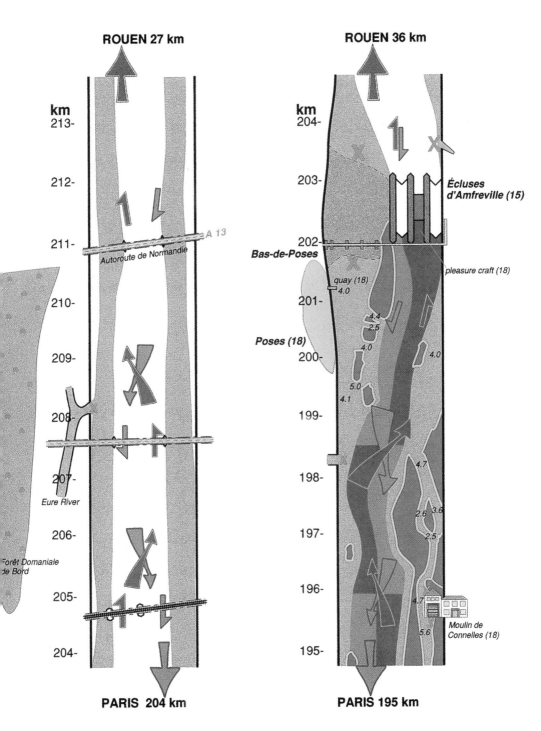

ROUEN 27 km

km
213-

212-

211-
Autoroute de Normandie — A 13

210-

209-

208-

207-
Eure River

206-

Forêt Domaniale
de Bord

205-

204-

PARIS 204 km

ROUEN 36 km

km
204-

203-
*Écluses
d'Amfreville (15)*

202-
Bas-de-Poses

quay (18)
4.0

pleasure craft (18)

201-
4.4
2.5

Poses (18)
200-
4.0
4.0

5.0
4.1

199-

198-
4.7

2.6 3.6

197-
2.5

196-
4.7

5.6
Moulin de
Connelles (18)

195-

PARIS 195 km

91

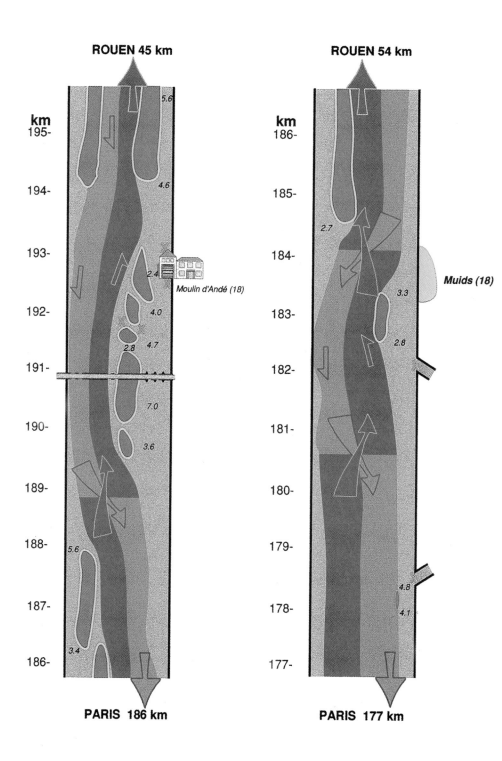

ROUEN 45 km

km
195-

194-

193-

192-

191-

190-

189-

188-

187-

186-

5.6

4.6

2.4

4.0

2.8   4.7

7.0

3.6

5.6

3.4

Moulin d'Andé *(18)*

PARIS 186 km

ROUEN 54 km

km
186-

185-

184-

183-

182-

181-

180-

179-

178-

177-

2.7

3.3

2.8

4.8

4.1

Muids (18)

PARIS 177 km

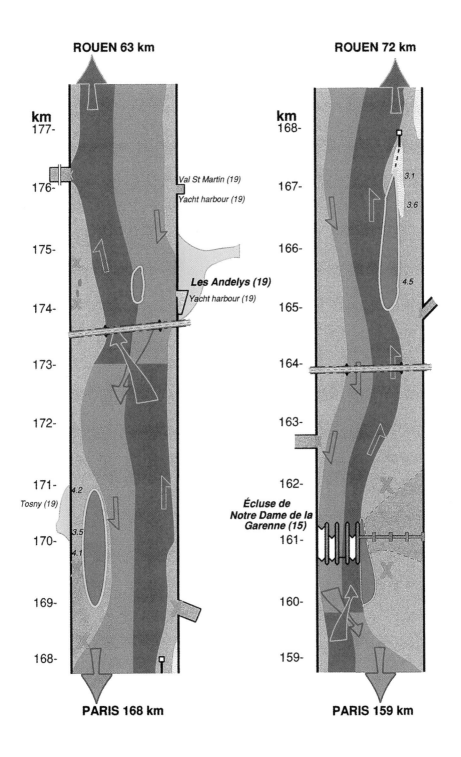

93

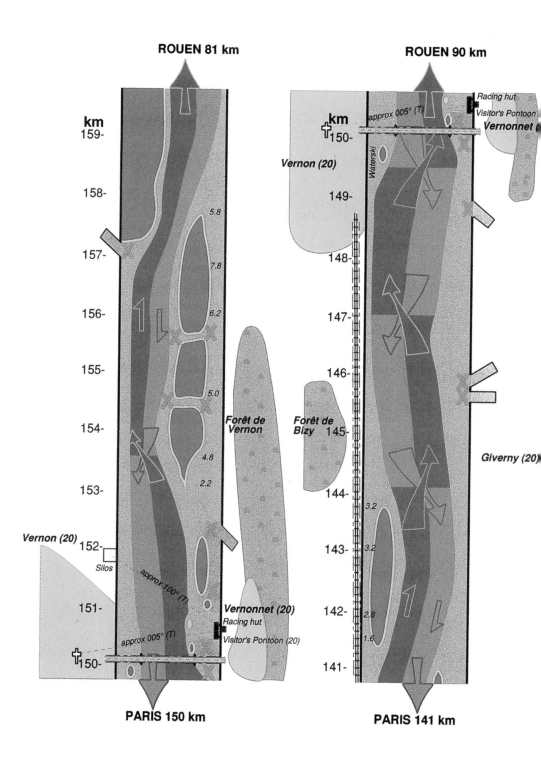

ROUEN 81 km

km
159-

158-

5.8

157-

7.8

156-

6.2

155-

5.0

154-

4.8

2.2

153-

Forêt de Vernon

Vernon (20) 152-

Silos

approx 100° (T)

151-

approx 005° (T)

150-

Vernonnet (20)
Racing hut
Visitor's Pontoon (20)

PARIS 150 km

ROUEN 90 km

Racing hut
Visitor's Pontoon
Vernonnet

km
150-
approx 005° (T)

Vernon (20)

149-

Waterski

148-

147-

146-

Forêt de Bizy 145-

Giverny (20)

144-

3.2

143-
3.2

142-
2.8

1.6

141-

PARIS 141 km

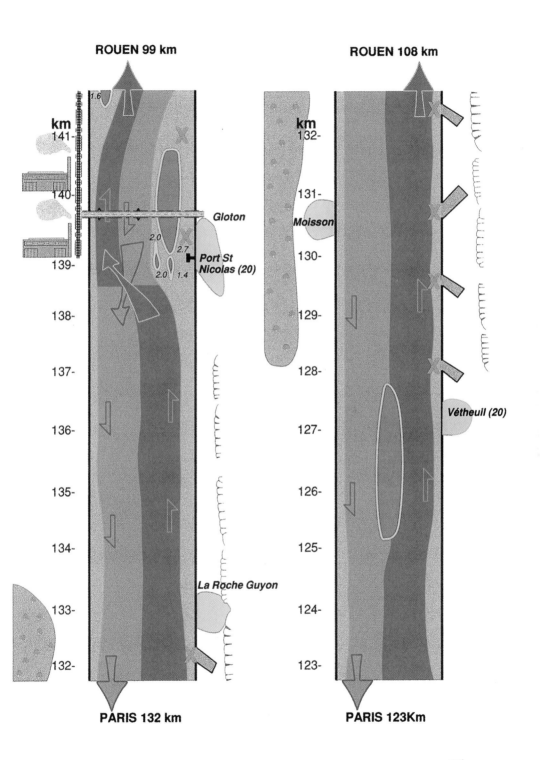

ROUEN 99 km

ROUEN 108 km

km
141-
140-
139-
138-
137-
136-
135-
134-
133-
132-

1.6

Gloton

2.0
2.7
2.0
1.4

Port St
Nicolas (20)

La Roche Guyon

PARIS 132 km

km
132-
131-
130-
129-
128-
127-
126-
125-
124-
123-

Moisson

Vétheuil (20)

PARIS 123Km

95

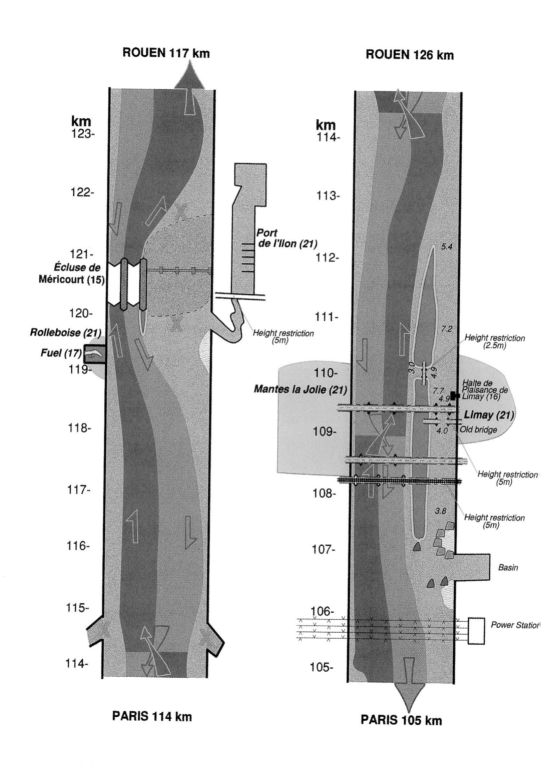

ROUEN 117 km

km
123-

122-

121-
Écluse de
Méricourt (15)

120-
Rolleboise (21)

Fuel (17)
119-

118-

117-

116-

115-

114-

Port
de l'Ilon (21)

Height restriction
(5m)

PARIS 114 km

ROUEN 126 km

km
114-

113-

112-

111-

110-
Mantes la Jolie (21)

109-

108-

107-

106-

105-

5.4

7.2

3.0 4.9

7.7
4.9

4.0

3.8

Height restriction
(2.5m)

Halte de
Plaisance de
Limay (16)

Limay (21)

Old bridge

Height restriction
(5m)

Height restriction
(5m)

Basin

Power Station

PARIS 105 km

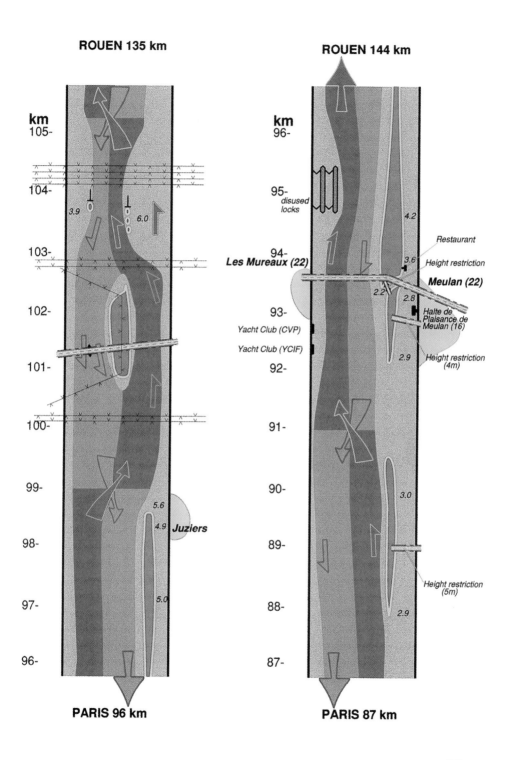

ROUEN 135 km

ROUEN 144 km

km
105-

km
96-

104-

3.9   6.0

95-
disused
locks

4.2

103-

Restaurant

94-
Les Mureaux (22)

3.6   Height restriction

Meulan (22)

102-

2.2   2.8

93-

Yacht Club (CVP)

Halte de
Plaisance de
Meulan (16)

Yacht Club (YCIF)

101-

92-

2.9   Height restriction
(4m)

100-

91-

99-

90-

3.0

5.6

98-

4.9 **Juziers**

89-

5.0

Height restriction
(5m)

97-

88-

2.9

96-

87-

PARIS 96 km

PARIS 87 km

97

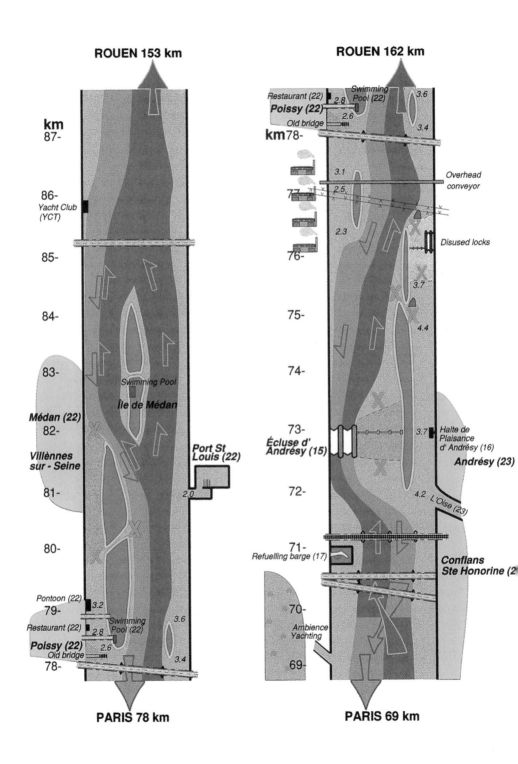

98

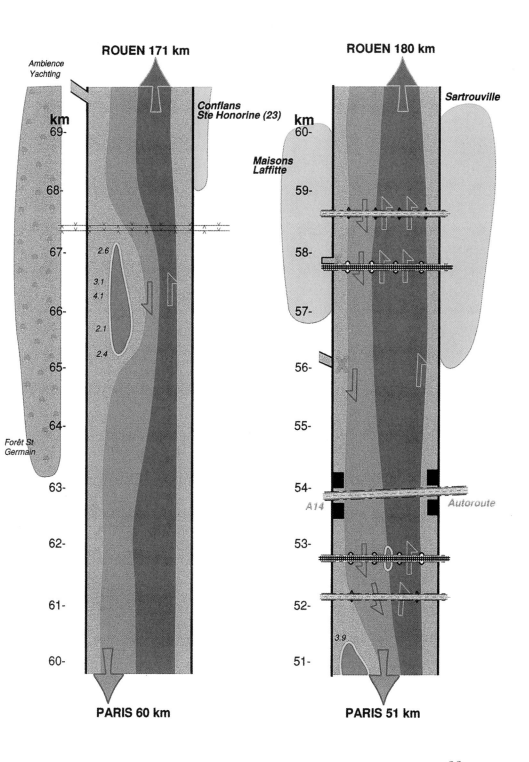

ROUEN 171 km

Ambience Yachting

km
69-

68-

67-

66-

65-

64-

Forêt St Germain

63-

62-

61-

60-

PARIS 60 km

Conflans Ste Honorine (23)

2.6
3.1
4.1
2.1
2.4

ROUEN 180 km

Sartrouville

km
60-

Maisons Laffitte

59-

58-

57-

56-

55-

54-

A14   *Autoroute*

53-

52-

51-

3.9

PARIS 51 km

99

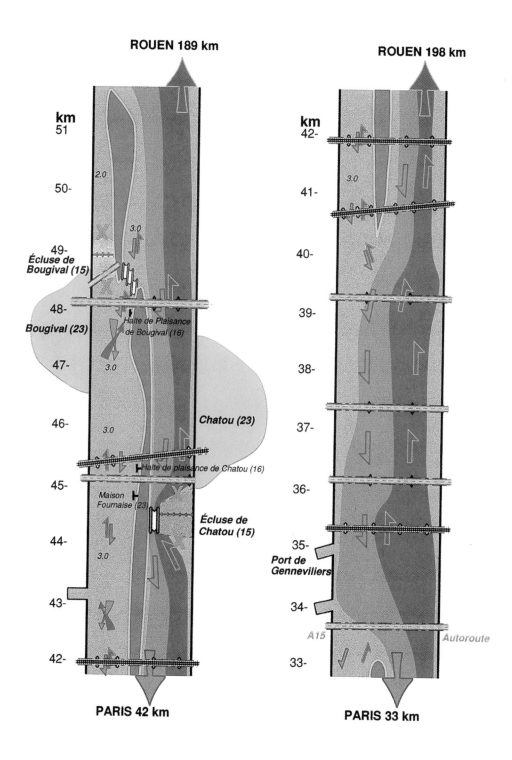

ROUEN 189 km

ROUEN 198 km

PARIS 42 km

PARIS 33 km

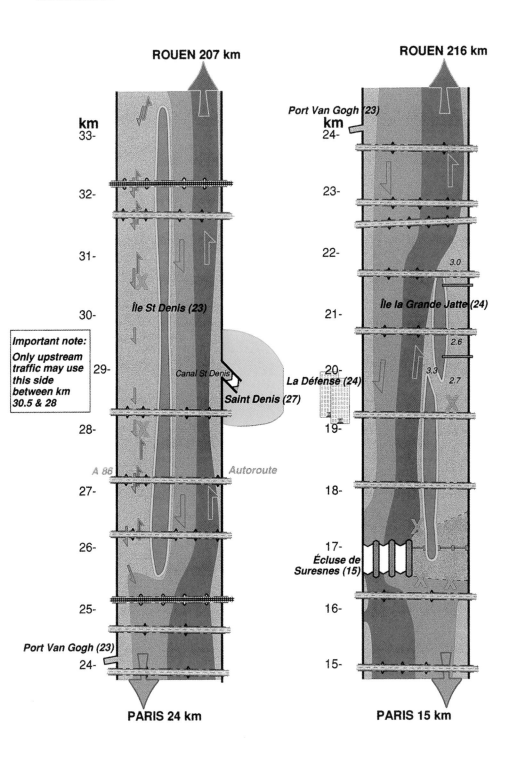

ROUEN 207 km

km
33-

32-

31-

30-

Île St Denis (23)

Important note:
Only upstream
traffic may use
this side
between km
30.5 & 28

29-

Canal St Denis

Saint Denis (27)

28-

A 86   *Autoroute*

27-

26-

25-

Port Van Gogh (23)
24-

PARIS 24 km

ROUEN 216 km

Port Van Gogh (23)
km
24-

23-

22-
3.0

Île la Grande Jatte (24)
21-
2.6
3.3
20-
2.7
La Défense (24)

19-

18-

17-
Écluse de
Suresnes (15)

16-

15-

PARIS 15 km

101

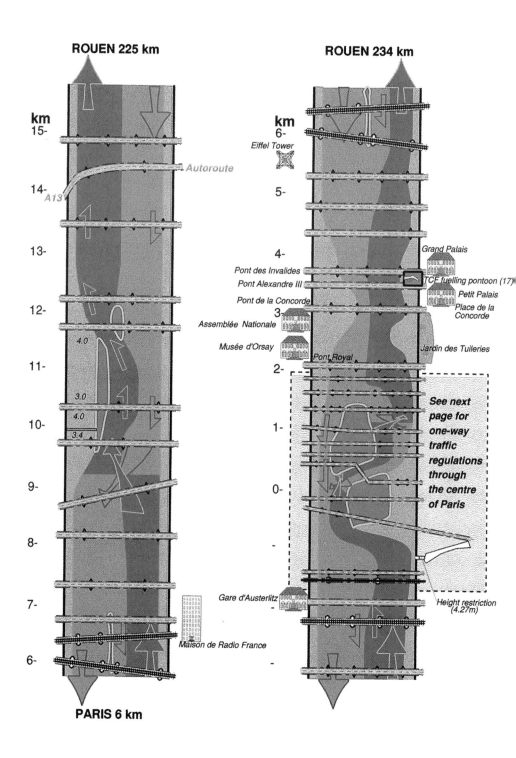

ROUEN 225 km

km
15-

14- A13

Autoroute

13-

12-

4.0

11-

3.0

4.0

10-

3.4

9-

8-

7-

6-

Maison de Radio France

PARIS 6 km

ROUEN 234 km

km
6-

Eiffel Tower

5-

4-

Grand Palais

Pont des Invalides

TCF fuelling pontoon (17)

Pont Alexandre III

Petit Palais

Pont de la Concorde

Place de la Concorde

Assemblée Nationale

3-

Musée d'Orsay

Jardin des Tuileries

Pont Royal

2-

See next page for one-way traffic regulations through the centre of Paris

1-

0-

Gare d'Austerlitz

Height restriction (4.27m)

7-

102

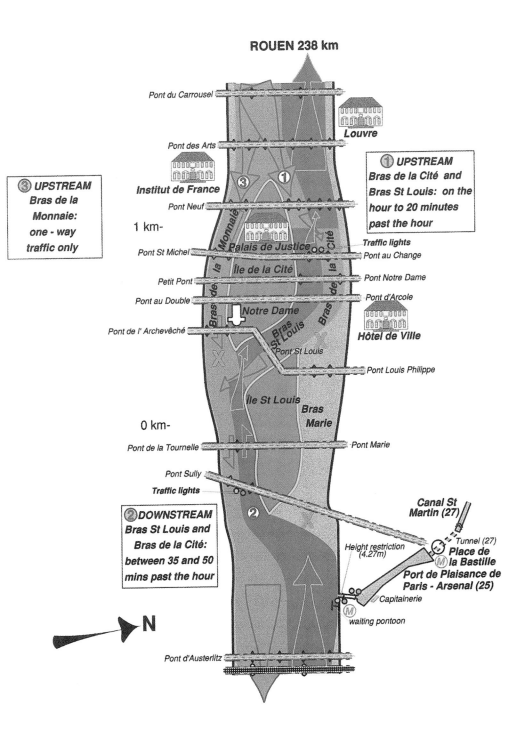

ROUEN 238 km

Pont du Carrousel

Louvre

Pont des Arts

③ UPSTREAM
Bras de la
Monnaie:
one - way
traffic only

Institut de France

① UPSTREAM
Bras de la Cité and
Bras St Louis: on the
hour to 20 minutes
past the hour

Pont Neuf

1 km-

Traffic lights

Pont au Change

Pont St Michel

Palais de Justice

Île de la Cité

Petit Pont

Pont Notre Dame

Pont au Double

Pont d'Arcole

Notre Dame

Hôtel de Ville

Pont de l' Archevêché

Bras
St Louis

Pont St Louis

Pont Louis Philippe

Ile St Louis

Bras
Marie

0 km-

Pont de la Tournelle

Pont Marie

Pont Sully

Traffic lights

② DOWNSTREAM
Bras St Louis and
Bras de la Cité:
between 35 and 50
mins past the hour

Canal St
Martin (27)

Tunnel (27)

Place de
la Bastille

Height restriction
(4.27m)

Port de Plaisance de
Paris - Arsenal (25)

Capitainerie

waiting pontoon

N

Pont d'Austerlitz

Appendix 1: An extended stay in France

Any boatowner contemplating a stay in France of longer than six months should make certain that both the person and the boat will not be liable for any taxes. Members of the RYA should seek advice from the Association.

The situation in 1997 was as follows:

- Boats owned and flagged outside the EU are entitled to remain in the EU as a temporary importation for six months of a 12 month period. Exceeding the six-month stay could involve taxes and possibly having to comply with certain French regulations in respect of licensing the boat.

- EU citizens staying more than 6 months in France with their boat may be considered French residents, requiring a form of boat passport which may involve paying French taxes.

Appendix 2: River signs

Follow the
direction indicated

Head for the
left-hand side of
the waterway

Head for the
right-hand side of
the waterway

Keep on the
left-hand side
of the canal

Keep on the
right-hand side
of the canal

Cross to the
left-hand side of
the waterway

Cross to the
right-hand side of
the waterway

Stop under
certain
conditions

Do not exceed
speed limit
(km/hr)

Sound horn

Extra vigilance
required

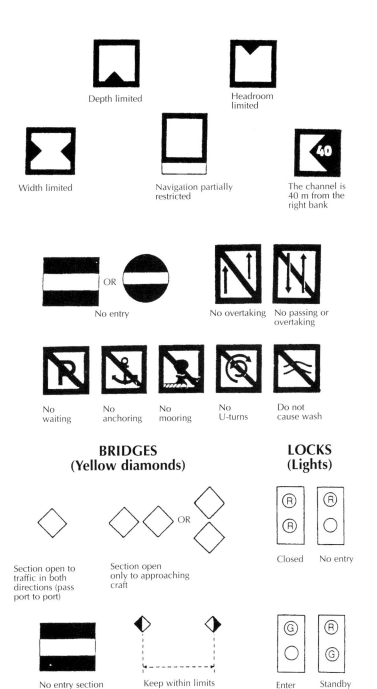

Depth limited

Headroom limited

Width limited

Navigation partially restricted

The channel is 40 m from the right bank

OR

No entry

No overtaking

No passing or overtaking

No waiting

No anchoring

No mooring

No U-turns

Do not cause wash

BRIDGES
(Yellow diamonds)

LOCKS
(Lights)

OR

Section open to traffic in both directions (pass port to port)

Section open only to approaching craft

Closed

No entry

No entry section

Keep within limits

Enter

Standby to enter

105

Index

Entries in italics indicate photographs.